Post-Achievement Depression

After the Summit: Finding Purpose When You've Already Made It

The Success Void - Rebuilding Identity Beyond Accomplishments

Nicci Brochard
&
Dr. Ben Chuba

Post-Achievement Depression

After the Summit: Finding Purpose When You've Already Made It

The Success Void - Rebuilding Identity Beyond Accomplishments

CROSSBORDER
PUBLISHERS LLC

New York, London, Quebec

Contents

Introduction

The rush of reaching the top, the thrill of achievement, and the overwhelming joy of success. There's nothing quite like it. You've worked tirelessly, endured countless sacrifices, and pushed through moments of doubt. And then, one day, you stand at the summit, looking down at all you've accomplished. You've "made it." But soon, something strange happens. The elation fades, and an unexpected emptiness sets in. It's as though the very thing you spent your life chasing no longer holds the same meaning.

This feeling, often dismissed or misunderstood, is what I call *Post-Achievement Depression*. After conquering your goals, after reaching that elusive summit of success, a void emerges—a quiet place where the external accolades no longer provide fulfillment. The applause fades, the applause that once fueled your ambitions, and now you're left wondering, "What's next?"

This book dives into that very space—the unsettling place between accomplishment and the next big thing. It's the journey of rediscovering purpose when it feels like you've already reached the peak, a path toward rebuilding your identity beyond just what you do or what you've achieved. Along this journey, we'll explore how to embrace a deeper sense of fulfillment that isn't reliant on accolades or validation.

Success isn't the destination—it's the beginning of something greater. The key lies in realizing that your life's meaning isn't tied solely to the peaks you've reached but to the infinite possibilities still before you. And with each new step, you'll find that the best is yet to come.

Nicci and I (Ben) are excited that you chose our book. You will not be disappointed. Thank you immensely.

Chapter 1

The Summit and the Void – Realizing You're Not Alone

A Story of the Unexpected Void

The stadium lights have dimmed and the confetti has settled. A celebrated champion sits alone in the quiet of her hotel room, gold medal in hand. Just yesterday, she stood on the podium with tears of joy as the world cheered. Friends toasted her victory late into the night. By all outward appearances, this was the pinnacle she had dreamed of. Yet this morning, as she opens her eyes, an unexpected hollowness weighs on her chest. Instead of lasting euphoria, she feels strangely *empty*. The long-awaited triumph that was supposed to fill her with pride has instead left her asking a frightening question: "Is this all there is?"

It's a narrative that might sound surprising, even counterintuitive. How could achieving a long-held goal – something that brought so much excitement and celebration – lead to an emotional void? To the outside world, our high achiever seems to have it all: the accolades, the success story, the public admiration. But internally, she experiences a quiet emptiness that she never anticipated. The truth is that her story is not an anomaly. It's a relatable tale shared by many high performers across different fields, from athletes and entertainers to entrepreneurs and scholars. Even at the summit of success, an unexpected void can await.

Consider the experience of Olympic swimming legend Michael Phelps. In 2004, at just 19 years old, Phelps achieved a historic haul of six gold and two bronze medals at the Athens Olympics. He should have been on top of the world. Yet he later admitted that as soon as the Games ended, he was hit by what he called "post-Olympic depression". After dedicating years of his life to a single goal, Phelps found himself suddenly asking, *"What the hell am I supposed to do? Where am I supposed to go? Who am I?"*. In his own words, reaching the pinnacle felt like standing *"at the top of the mountain"* only to realize he had lost his sense of direction and self. Our imaginary champion's void is the very real feeling Phelps and countless others have faced: a jarring emptiness when the initial high of achievement fades.

The story of this unexpected void helps set the stage for our exploration. It shows that even after reaching a life summit — whether it's winning an Olympic medal, acing a huge project, or celebrating a career milestone — one can wake up the next day not with elation but with confusion and melancholy. By starting with this narrative, we shine a light on a hidden truth: if you have ever felt deflated or empty after a big win, you are far from alone. This opening story may be fictionalized, but it encapsulates a very real phenomenon that high achievers around the world quietly experience.

When the Applause Fades

The moment of victory often comes with a roar of applause, a flood of congratulations, and an adrenaline rush of joy. But what happens after the applause fades and the audience goes home? In that silence, many

4

achievers confront a stark contrast between *public celebration* and *private emotion*. The project is delivered, the award is in hand, the hard work is finally over – and yet a sense of hollowness creeps in once the celebrations end. It's in those solitary moments, perhaps lying awake in bed after the big day, that a champion or high achiever might think, "Why don't I feel happier?"

Psychologists sometimes refer to this as the "post-success hangover" – the emotional comedown after the high of achievement. During the build-up, every moment was filled with purpose: training for the competition, preparing for the product launch, writing the final chapters of the thesis. But now the structured routine and the thrill of anticipation have vanished. What replaces them can be a disorienting void. As one writer described it, achieving a major goal can leave us with a *"purpose vacuum"* — a gap where our sense of direction used to be. The cheering crowd is gone, and so is the clear next step. In this vacuum, uncertainty and aimlessness can take hold.

For our Olympic champion, the quiet hotel room the next morning feels almost alien. Yesterday everyone told her how proud and happy she must be. Today she wonders why she feels *none* of that. The contrast between the external fanfare and her internal confusion makes her feel guilty and bewildered: *Shouldn't I be happy right now?* This scenario is strikingly common. Athletes often report an emotional low after big events; in fact, sports psychologists note that many Olympians experience a "period of letdown" once the Games conclude. One study found that about 24% of Olympic and Paralympic athletes reported significant psychological distress in the months after the competition. With the medals won and the spotlight turned off, these athletes suddenly face the question of *"What now?"*, often accompanied by a loss of identity and direction. The phenomenon is so prevalent that it's informally dubbed the "post-Olympic blues."

This letdown isn't limited to sports. Entrepreneurs have described finishing a successful startup exit or major project only to feel unexpectedly listless once the intense work is done. Students finishing a degree, or artists releasing a career-defining album, can all encounter that same unsettling quiet after the climax. The applause – literal or figurative – fades, and with it goes the structure and excitement that drove them forward. The high achiever is left alone with their thoughts, and those thoughts often turn introspective and even bleak. In private, they may grapple with questions like, *"Why am I not happier? Is there something wrong with me?"* The world around them expects them to be celebrating, which only heightens the sense of isolation.

By exploring this after-the-summit silence, we validate a powerful truth: the emotional crash after success is real. The juxtaposition of public joy and private emptiness can be confusing and painful, but it is also a normal human response. When the applause fades, it reveals the raw, unfiltered feelings that achievement alone may not erase. If you have ever felt a creeping emptiness right when you thought you'd be happiest, know that this quiet moment of doubt has echoed in the minds of many others who have walked across life's biggest stages.

Naming the Feeling

It might come as a relief to learn that psychologists actually have a name for this perplexing post-victory melancholy. It's been termed "post-achievement depression." Far from being a personal failing or an odd quirk, this emotional slump after a major accomplishment is a recognized phenomenon. Post-achievement depression involves experiencing a sense of purposelessness or sadness after completing a long-standing goal. In other words, that numbing emptiness and lack of motivation that often follow a big win are *not* just "in your head" – they're a documented response that many people experience. Psychologists reassure us that there is nothing inherently "wrong" with you if you feel this way. Achieving a dream can trigger a complex mix of emotions: exhaustion, restlessness, frustration, self-doubt, melancholy, even a subtle sense of existential crisis. The mind and body have been on overdrive, and once the finish line is crossed, it's common for them to hit a psychological brick wall.

Crucially, this post-summit blues is common across all walks of life. It doesn't discriminate between an Olympic gold medalist, a newly minted PhD, a CEO who just sold her company, or a parent who successfully organized a huge family event. Students concluding their studies, writers typing "The End" on a manuscript, office workers securing a hard-won promotion, or athletes concluding a long season – all can feel this emotional downturn. The aftermath of achievement *"knows no bounds"*; it's a shared human experience that resonates across diverse paths and pursuits. By naming the feeling, we take the first step toward understanding it. Just as naming an illness can bring relief that one is not "just imagining things," recognizing *post-achievement depression* as a real phenomenon can bring a sense of validation. *You are not the only one, and you are certainly not "ungrateful" or "broken" for feeling this way.*

Why does this happen? Psychology offers a few insightful explanations. One is the idea of the "arrival fallacy." Coined by positivity researcher Tal Ben-Shahar, the arrival fallacy is the false belief that once we *arrive* at a certain goal or milestone, we will attain enduring happiness. We often pin our hopes on the idea that *"I'll be happy when I get there"* – when I win that award, earn that amount, achieve that status. But as Ben-Shahar and others point out, this is an *oversimplification* of how human happiness works. We adapt quickly to our achievements; the glow of fulfillment often doesn't last as long as we expect. In our champion's case, she assumed a gold medal would equate to lifelong pride and contentment. In reality, while the victory brought a burst of joy, it didn't fix every insecurity or fill every void in her life. The anticipated *happy-ever-after* proved fleeting. Many of us have experienced a version of this: getting the new job or the new house or the big prize, only to find that our baseline mood returns and the same old doubts creep back. The arrival wasn't a permanent paradise after all.

Biology plays a role as well. Neuroscientists have observed that our brains are essentially hardwired to enjoy the chase more than the catch. During the pursuit of a goal, our brain's reward chemical – dopamine – fires up, giving us energy and focus. Each incremental step toward the goal releases dopamine that propels us forward. We feel *alive* when we are striving: late nights in the office, intense practice sessions, all fueled by a neurochemical push that says this effort has meaning. However, when we finally hit our target, that neurochemical thrill can evaporate rather quickly. The same dopamine that made the journey exhilarating drops off sharply once the journey is over. As one research psychologist explained, *"once we hit our target, the rewards may be short-lived, leaving us bereft of the thrill we experienced when pursuing our initial goal."* In simpler terms, the joy was in the journey, and now that the journey is complete, our brain is left with a void where the chase used to be. This sudden vacuum can manifest as listlessness or depression. It's a bit like the "runner's high" that collapses into fatigue when the race is finished. Understanding this biological pattern can be reassuring: the flat feeling after a triumph isn't because the goal was wrong or because you're impossible to satisfy – it can be an *inbuilt chemical response* in the brain coming down from a long-term high.

By naming post-achievement depression and understanding concepts like the arrival fallacy and the dopamine crash, we start to see that the "success void" has logical causes. Importantly, knowing these feelings are *normal* and *expected* in many cases can remove the sting of self-blame. You're not "failing at being happy"; you're experiencing a known psychological cycle. Many high achievers quietly go through this, even if they don't talk about it openly. The irony is that the moments that look like ultimate victories on the outside can internally be times of profound vulnerability. The mind and body need time to recalibrate after the summit. Recognizing this experience for what it is – a temporary emotional slump that often follows intense effort – allows us to approach it with more compassion and less judgment toward ourselves.

Not Alone at the Top

Perhaps the most comforting insight of all is this: you are not alone at the top. The sense of emptiness after success is something even the most famous and accomplished figures have candidly acknowledged. It may be comforting (and a bit astonishing) to realize that the very people society idolizes for "having it all" have also felt that void. Let's look at a few powerful examples from modern history and pop culture that illustrate how common this experience really is.

In the world of sports, consider legendary NFL quarterback Tom Brady, who is often deemed the greatest of all time in his sport. At the time Brady had "only" three Super Bowl rings (he would eventually earn seven), he gave an interview that revealed a deep sense of searching. *"Why do I have three Super Bowl rings and still think there's something greater out there for me?"* he wondered aloud. *"I reached my goal, my dream, my life. Me, I think: 'God, it's gotta be more than this.'"* This startling admission came from a man who had achieved more on the football field than anyone could imagine. Brady's words "It's gotta be more than this" encapsulate the success void perfectly – even standing at the pinnacle of his career, he felt a gnawing sense that something was missing.

Hollywood offers similar stories. Brad Pitt, one of the most successful and recognizable film stars in the world, has spoken about the disillusionment that can accompany fame and achievement. *"I know all these things are supposed to seem important to us — the car, the condo, our version of success,"* Pitt said in an interview, *"but if that's the case, why is the general feeling out there reflecting more impotence and isolation and desperation and loneliness?"* Despite his wealth and awards, Pitt sensed a *"numbing of the soul"* beneath the surface of modern success. In other words, all the external markers of achievement weren't delivering the inner fulfillment one might expect. His candid observation that society's image of success often leads to *"a dead end, a numbing of the soul, a complete atrophy of the spiritual being"* is a stark reminder that external success doesn't automatically translate to inner peace.

Pop music and film icon Lady Gaga shared a related sentiment after one of the most spectacular runs of success imaginable. In a short span, Gaga had top-selling albums, won Grammy Awards, performed at the Super Bowl halftime show, and even earned an Academy Award for her acting. Yet, she confessed that *"I won an Oscar, I sang at the Super Bowl, but in some ways I still feel empty inside."* Achievements that few could ever dream of accomplishing still left her searching: *"I think it's because I'm still searching for who I am and where I fit in.".* Gaga's honesty highlights an important point: success can mask the ongoing journey of self-discovery, but it cannot replace it. She had reached the stars professionally, but personally she still needed purpose and identity beyond those trophies. The fact that an artist of her caliber could feel *empty* after such triumphs speaks volumes — it tells every reader who feels let down after their own success that feeling empty doesn't mean you failed to appreciate your achievement; it means you're human.

Even the world of music stardom has its tales of post-summit blues. Consider Liam Payne, member of the wildly successful boy band One Direction. The group sold tens of millions of records and achieved global fame in their youth. Yet Payne has spoken about how his life felt like it was spiraling out of control during and after those peak years. Despite the adoration of fans worldwide, he described loneliness and recklessness behind the scenes. *"Once people get to the top, they realize there is nothing there,"* an article poignantly noted about the emptiness that can follow massive success. Payne's struggles with substances and mental health, culminating in personal crises, illustrate how the view from the top can be lonely and frightening, contradicting all expectations.

The sense of void at the summit isn't a new discovery of the 21st century either – it's been a part of the human condition for ages. Historical figures and philosophers have wrestled with it. An often-cited example is King Solomon, the ancient Israelite king famed for his wisdom and wealth. According to biblical tradition, Solomon had unparalleled riches, power, and accomplishments; yet in the Book of Ecclesiastes he reflected that it was all meaningless and empty in the end. *"I looked at everything I had worked so hard to accomplish, and it was all so meaningless – like chasing the wind,"* he lamented in ancient scripture. This echoes through time as a reminder that the feeling of the "emptiness of achievement" is profoundly human and age-old. When even a king who "had it all" recognized a void, it underscores that the issue transcends eras and contexts.

More recently, actress Halle Berry made history with a career-defining triumph – winning the Academy Award for Best Actress in 2002, the first Black woman ever to do so. It was a moment of public glory and significance. Yet Berry later revealed that in the wake of her Oscar win, she fell into a difficult period of depression. The world saw her achievement; what they didn't see was her private struggle with mood and meaning. Berry's openness about how a pinnacle achievement coincided with emotional challenges has helped destigmatize this experience. It shows that even when life's biggest dream comes true, one's mental health doesn't magically become invincible. Success and sadness can coexist, even at the highest peak of one's career. By sharing her story, Berry reinforced the message that no one is immune to these feelings – not even an Oscar-winning superstar.

And of course, we must return to Michael Phelps, whose story opened this chapter. After his record-smashing Olympic victories, Phelps struggled deeply, even contemplating suicide at one point in the years following his wins. It took therapy and a reevaluation of his life beyond swimming for him to heal and find a new purpose. Phelps eventually discovered that he had to view himself as more than just "the swimmer" – he had to find Michael the person, not defined solely by gold medals. His journey underscores a vital lesson: when an identity has been built around achievement, reaching the goal can feel like losing oneself, unless we prepare to build a broader sense of self.

All of these examples, from star athletes and entertainers to historical figures, drive home a unifying truth: If you've ever reached a goal only to find it didn't bring the lasting satisfaction you expected, you are far from the only one. In fact, you're in the company of some of the most accomplished people in the world. The post-achievement void does not discriminate by fame, fortune, or level of success. It is *human*. Knowing this creates a compassionate connection. You can take heart that behind many smiling podium photographs and victory speeches, there may lie private doubts similar to your own. This chapter is here to normalize that experience – to tell you that feeling this void is not a sign of weakness or ingratitude, but a common psychological phase that many go through.

Looking at the summit and the void together, we begin to see the full picture: the incredible high of achievement and the often-unspoken low that can follow. By recognizing this pattern and hearing the voices of those who have lived it, we validate our own feelings and strip away the stigma. You are *not* failing at happiness; you are navigating a nuanced emotional journey that success can trigger. Standing at the top can indeed feel lonely – but in truth, you're not alone in feeling that way. In the chapters to come, we will delve deeper into why this happens and, more importantly, how to find renewed purpose and identity beyond your accomplishments. For now, take comfort in this knowledge: the summit may come with a void, but together, we've named it, understood it, and realized we're not alone in it. That understanding is the first step on the path to filling that void with something more enduring and meaningful, now that you've already "made it" to the top.

Chapter 2

The High After the High – Why Success Can Feel Empty

Imagine standing at the pinnacle of your greatest achievement – the moment you've worked for, dreamed of, and sacrificed for. You expect to feel on top of the world. Yet, once the initial celebration fades, an unexpected emptiness creeps in. Olympic champions have described this phenomenon: after the medals are won and the cheering stops, life suddenly feels ordinary again. Multi-millionaire entrepreneurs, upon selling their companies, often wake up the next day feeling strangely aimless. Even legendary figures have voiced this sentiment. After winning three Super Bowls by age 27, quarterback Tom Brady famously asked, "Is this all there is?" He had reached the summit of success in his sport, yet he was left wondering what more life had to offer. This perplexing letdown after a victory is more common than people realize. In this chapter, we delve into why achieving a long-sought goal can leave us feeling deflated. We explore the chemical highs and lows in our brains, the psychological illusions of lasting joy, the collision of expectations with reality, and the very normal "success hangover" that often follows a big win. By understanding why success can feel empty, we can learn to cope with that void and find renewed purpose beyond the trophy moment.

Chasing the High

The pursuit of a goal can be exhilarating, sometimes even more thrilling than achieving the goal itself. Modern neuroscience helps explain this paradox. As we chase an ambition – whether it's building a business, training for a marathon, or writing a book – our brain continually rewards us with feel-good chemicals. Dopamine, often nicknamed the "motivation molecule," surges during the process of striving. Each small win along the way – every completed task or milestone reached – triggers a dopamine release that fuels excitement and drive. It's nature's way of propelling us forward. Think of how you feel when you're closing in on a target: energized, focused, even euphoric. A student pulling an all-nighter to finish a thesis, or an artist absorbed in creating their masterpiece, might feel a vibrant intensity that pushes them on. This is the brain's reward system at work, keeping us in the hunt with a neurochemical high.

Notably, dopamine is more about anticipation than the actual reward. Research by neuroscientists like Professor Robert Sapolsky has shown that dopamine spikes in expectation of a reward rather than at the moment of receiving it. In other words, our brains light up while we're waiting for the prize, climbing the mountain, more than when we finally stand at the summit. Stanford's Andrew Huberman, a neuroscientist who studies human performance, has popularized this idea: the pursuit – the journey – is what gives us that electric buzz of motivation. It's why a mountain climber feels most alive during the climb, not necessarily at the peak. Or why an entrepreneur feels on fire in the hectic days of building a startup, more than on the day they sell the company. The chase itself is thrilling and purpose-filled.

However, when we finally hit our target, the brain's chemistry shifts dramatically. Finishing the goal brings a brief surge of dopamine and endorphins – that rush of pride and relief when you cross the finish line or hold your award. Yet immediately after, those neurochemical levels drop off sharply. The high that was sustaining us can vanish almost overnight. Psychologically and biologically, we come down from the "chase high." If you've ever felt a bit low or listless in the days after a big win, that is your brain recalibrating from a dopamine peak back to normal levels. Some researchers even say it can dip *below* normal for a while, as if your brain used up its reserves of happy chemicals during the sprint and needs time to refuel. What you experience is essentially a chemical comedown. One moment you're basking in achievement, and shortly after you're confronting a void where all that forward-driving energy used to be.

This understanding can be eye-opening: the elation of accomplishment is often chemically short-lived. It's not that your triumph lacked value – our biology simply isn't designed to keep us in a constant state of euphoria. We're wired to strive. Once there's nothing to strive for, the brain's reward machinery idles, and we *feel* that shift deeply. An athlete might describe it as the silence after the roar of the crowd – suddenly, there's quiet. The everyday world, which you might have tuned out during the all-consuming pursuit, comes back into focus and feels strangely dull. People sometimes chase bigger and bigger goals for this very reason: they're seeking another hit of that pursuit-fueled excitement. But understanding the role of brain chemistry reminds us that no high can last indefinitely. The dopamine rush was never meant to be permanent; it's a temporary fuel. Hence the old adage rings true: the journey matters more than the destination itself. The journey is where our brain finds its joy.

The Arrival Fallacy – Illusion of Lasting Joy

During the long climb toward success, many of us hold a powerful illusion: once I *arrive* at my goal, I will be happy **forever**. Psychologists have a name for this mistaken belief – the arrival fallacy. Coined by Dr. Tal Ben-Shahar, a Harvard-trained expert on happiness, the arrival fallacy is the conviction that achieving a certain milestone (landing the dream job, earning a fortune, winning an award) will bring enduring bliss and solve all our problems. It's the "I'll be happy when..." syndrome. We imagine the promotion or the gold medal will usher in a permanent state of contentment. From a distance, that finish line gleams like a promised land where all our struggles finally make sense.

Reality, however, often tells a different story. Ben-Shahar observed that many high achievers – from celebrities to CEOs – reach their long-awaited victory only to find the happiness boost is fleeting. Almost like a mirage, the satisfaction fades after a short while, and life returns to its previous baseline of emotions. The big trophy doesn't magically fix lingering personal issues, heal our insecurities, or fill every void in our hearts. A star athlete might still struggle with anxiety or loneliness after the championship parade is over. A newly-minted millionaire may find that money solved some practical problems but didn't deliver meaning or self-worth. The external achievement, impressive as it is, does not permanently transform the inner landscape of our feelings.

In fact, chasing permanent joy through accomplishments can set us up for disappointment. When we pin all our hopes on one goal, we load it with unrealistic expectations. Tal Ben-Shahar and other psychologists point out that this illusion has tripped up countless successful people. Consider the stories of those who seemingly "had it all" yet still found themselves unhappy. We've seen famous entertainers and business magnates succumb to depression or burnout even after reaching the heights of success. Why? One reason is that the long-term happiness they expected success to provide didn't materialize; the issues they had before were still there after the applause died down. Comedian Jim Carrey, who achieved wealth and global fame, once remarked that he wished everyone could be rich and famous so they would see it's not the answer to happiness. His words echo a sobering truth: achieving your dreams won't automatically make you eternally happy.

Psychological research supports this. Studies in positive psychology suggest that external circumstances (like income, awards, status) have surprisingly limited impact on our overall happiness in the long run. We humans quickly adapt to good fortune – a phenomenon known as hedonic adaptation. The new car becomes ordinary after a few months; the thrill of a promotion wears off as the job becomes routine; even a mansion can start to feel like just another house once it's your everyday environment. In essence, we return to our usual happiness set-point. So if we believed that reaching a goal would lock in a permanent state of joy, we experience a rude awakening: the joy is temporary, and then normal life resumes. This isn't to say goals have no value – far from it. It means that pinning all our hopes on a singular achievement to fix everything is an illusion. By recognizing the arrival fallacy, we understand that while accomplishing something can certainly boost our happiness, that boost is naturally short-term. Lasting fulfillment has to come from something deeper and more continuous than one moment of victory.

Expectations vs. Reality

A big part of why success can feel empty lies in the gap between our expectations and reality. In our minds, we often script a perfect ending: crossing that finish line will feel like pure bliss; achieving this goal will make us feel complete and set life right. We dream about the moment for so long that it swells in our imagination. But when the anticipated moment finally arrives, it rarely matches that idealized vision. The celebration might be brief or muted. Friends and family cheer for a day, then everyone goes back to their lives. You wake up the next morning after the big achievement, and the world looks surprisingly the same. The bills still need to be paid, the laundry still needs doing, and you're still the same person – just with a trophy on the shelf or a new title by your name. The contrast between what we imagined and what we actually experience can be stark.

This dissonance can provoke a profound inner question: "Is this all there is?" We expect a triumphant finale and find instead that life keeps unfolding with its usual complexities. Tom Brady's candid reflection after winning multiple championships captures this sentiment. After reaching a pinnacle that most people only dream of, Brady admitted he thought, "God, there's got to be more than this." Here was a man with multiple Super Bowl rings, wealth, and acclaim, yet he felt a surprising lack of fulfillment. His honest question – *What else is there?* – reveals how success can lay bare a certain emptiness that achievement was supposed to erase. We might not all be sports legends, but many can relate in smaller ways: the college graduate who expected euphoria on commencement day but instead feels anxious and uncertain about the future, or the artist who releases an album and immediately wonders why they're not as happy as they imagined they'd be. The finish line, once crossed, often shifts into a new starting line of questions and soul-searching.

There's also a sense of loss that accompanies reaching a goal, which we seldom anticipate. For months or years, the goal was your guiding star. It occupied your thoughts, structured your routine, gave your life direction. Once it's achieved, that driving force vanishes. The grand project that consumed your days is done, and its absence can leave a void. It's a bit like a traveler who's reached the destination and suddenly misses the long journey. A novelist might spend years immersed in writing a book, and after publication, feel empty because the epic creative quest is over. The reality of success is that it often marks an ending as much as a beginning. But we tend to focus only on what we'll gain (happiness, pride, recognition) and not on what we might lose (purpose, a daily mission, the excitement of progress). When reality doesn't live up to our high expectations, disappointment is natural. This isn't a sign of ingratitude or personal failure; it's a common human experience. By understanding this gap between expectation and reality, we can be kinder to ourselves when the big moment doesn't feel perfect. Instead of thinking, "Something is wrong with me for not being overjoyed," we can acknowledge that our mind's fantasy was just that – a fantasy. Real life, even at the summit of success, is still real life, with all its imperfections and mixed emotions. Armed with this awareness, we can adjust our perspective for future goals, aiming for excellence but not assuming that achievement alone will create a perfect state of bliss.

The Success Hangover

Perhaps the most reassuring insight of all is that the "down" you feel after a "high" is completely normal. In fact, it's so common that it has earned a nickname: *the success hangover.* Just as an evening of celebration with too many drinks can lead to a morning of headache and fatigue, an intense period of striving followed by victory can lead to an emotional and physical crash. This is essentially a hangover of accomplishment. After the adrenaline rush subsides and the dopamine party in your brain winds down, you experience a natural low. Energy that ran hot now runs cold. Elation can flip to blues. It may be disorienting – you think you *should* be happy, yet emotionally you feel drained or flat. But knowing that there are biological and psychological reasons for this crash can help remove the stigma and reduce the surprise.

High achievers from all walks of life have openly talked about this phenomenon, which helps normalize it. Even astronauts after a historic mission have reported a deep void upon returning to Earth—after the unimaginable high of walking on the Moon, ordinary life back home felt oddly trivial in comparison. Soldiers returning home from the intensity of a mission, students after graduating, performers after a major concert tour, or even parents after the whirlwind of a big wedding – all can feel a version of this crash. Olympic gold medalist Michael Phelps, for example, has spoken about the "post-Olympic blues" that hit him and many fellow athletes after the Games. In one documentary, Phelps estimated that about 80% of Olympians experience some form of depression once the Olympic high is over. These are the best athletes in the world – people who seem invincible and on top of life – yet they often find themselves in a funk once the big event is behind them. Phelps described finishing the Olympics and suddenly feeling "lost," asking himself, "Who am I outside of the pool?" His body and mind had been pushed to extremes in pursuit of gold; when that mission was accomplished, he was left with exhaustion and a daunting open space ahead. It's a dramatic example, but even on a more ordinary level we see this pattern.

Crucially, the success hangover is a phase, not a permanent condition. It's the mind and body's way of recuperating and recalibrating. Knowing this can be immensely comforting. Rather than feeling guilty about being down ("I achieved something great – I'm supposed to be happy, what's wrong with me?"), we can accept that a recovery period is natural and even necessary. It's okay to feel a bit blue or disoriented after a major life event – even a positive one. In fact, psychologists note that even joyful milestones (weddings, births, big accomplishments) can bring a bout of melancholy as life shifts to a new chapter. The key is to frame it as a temporary comedown and to treat ourselves kindly during this time. Just as you might nurse a physical hangover with rest and hydration, an emotional hangover calls for patience and self-care. Some people find it helps to talk with others who have been through similar experiences – you'll discover it's incredibly common and that you're not alone. Others channel the restless energy into gentle activities: go for walks, reconnect with hobbies, give yourself permission to relax and recharge a bit. Over time, that emotional fog will lift.

Understanding the success hangover also means we can prepare for it. We can anticipate that after any summit, there will be a descent. That doesn't mean we should avoid striving for big goals; it means we should plan for the after just as we plan for the climb. In practical terms, this might involve having a new sense of purpose ready to embrace once one goal is done – not necessarily jumping immediately into the next rat race, but gradually finding the next meaningful challenge or project so that we continue to have direction. It might also mean focusing on parts of life that give steady fulfillment, like relationships, personal growth, or helping others, especially in the lull after a big achievement. Many thinkers and achievers have noted that true happiness comes from those ongoing sources, not one-time events. As the haze of the hangover clears, it becomes an opportunity: a chance to reflect on what truly matters to you beyond the applause of accomplishment.

In sum, feeling empty after success doesn't mean there's something wrong with you or that your success was pointless. It's a human experience with biological underpinnings and psychological roots. By learning about the dopamine-fueled high of the chase, the arrival fallacy that promises more than reality can give, the inevitable gap between expectation and reality, and the very normal success hangover, you gain insight into your own post-achievement emotions. Most importantly, you can be kinder to yourself. Instead of seeing the post-summit blues as a personal failing, you can recognize them as a natural part of the cycle of achievement. The summit, after all, is just one point on a longer journey. After the summit, the path continues – down, around, and onward to other peaks and valleys.

For many, this unsettling void after success can become the start of a new journey – an opportunity to discover deeper meaning and redefine what success means in your life. When you've already "made it," you now have the chance to explore broader horizons of purpose and fulfillment beyond any single summit.

In the next chapters, we will explore how to navigate that path: how to rebuild identity beyond your accomplishments and discover fulfillment that endures long after the thrill of victory.

Chapter 3

Identity Lost and Found – You Are More Than Your Achievement

When Success Becomes Identity

It's surprisingly easy for our sense of self to become entangled with our accomplishments. High achievers often wear their titles and trophies like crowns, believing that what they **are** (CEO, Olympian, award-winner) is who they are. Modern culture reinforces this: we spend nearly a third of our lives working, so jobs naturally shape identity. When people ask, "What do you do?", they're really probing *who* you are, and many of us respond by pointing to roles or accolades. Over time, this can blur the line between our work selves and our true selves. Psychologists warn that when personal identity becomes fused with career or success, it creates a fragile foundation. For a while, it can feel empowering – wearing your success as a badge of worth – but it also means any change or loss in that arena strikes at the core of your self-worth. In clinical psychologist Sabrina Romanoff's words, "If your self-worth is tied to what you do then all outcomes will influence your self-perception," so even a normal setback can trigger a *"crisis in identity"*. This enmeshment makes you *vulnerable* to painful shocks if the title is stripped away or the applause stops. Many who have climbed high find themselves asking: without this achievement, what remains of *me*?

The Post-Goal Identity Crisis

Finishing a defining goal can feel like suddenly wandering off a cliff. When life has revolved around reaching a summit, arriving at the top can provoke an unsettling question: *Who am I now?* Achievers often go from the rush of purpose to a jarring sense of disorientation once the mission is complete. Psychologists recognize this as a common phenomenon called post-achievement depression – a period of purposelessness or sadness after completing a long-standing goal. Far from being rare, this experience spans all walks of life. Graduates completing degrees, writers typing "The End" on a manuscript, professionals earning a promotion, entrepreneurs selling their startup, athletes retiring from competition – all can feel that numb emptiness after the celebration fades. Success, ironically, can shake your identity as much as failure. If your self-definition was heavily tied to a pursuit, its completion can leave you uncertain about your role and direction. One moment you had a clear purpose; the next, that guiding star is gone. In elite sports this is so common it's dubbed the "Olympic blues" – the depression Olympians feel when the Games are over and they're "not quite sure what to do with themselves". Retirement or goal completion often means a loss of the structure and meaning that anchored one's days. Indeed, a Psychology Today report notes that retirement can lead many high-achievers to feel a profound loss of meaning and even an identity crisis, as they question who they are without that previous role. It's important to stress that if you're thinking *"Who am I now?"* after a big success, you're not alone. This unnerving identity shakiness is a natural reaction when one's defining goal – the very axis of one's identity – suddenly vanishes.

The Vacuum of Purpose

Perhaps the most unsettling aspect of great achievement is the *"now what?"* feeling that follows a big win. Many achievers expect to feel lasting fulfillment at the summit, only to find a void. The driving force that propelled them for years is suddenly gone, leaving a vacuum of purpose. Instead of victorious contentment, they experience being unmoored – as if a ship that finally reached port now finds its anchor lifted again. Psychologists describe this aftermath as a "purpose vacuum," where the structure, motivation, and sense of mission that once filled one's life suddenly evaporate. Until a new direction is found, that void can bring real sorrow and listlessness. Legendary comedian Jim Carrey, after accumulating wealth and fame, observed this hollow feeling. Each time he achieved a new hit, he would think, "Yeah, it was a fantastic hit, but what now?" – eventually realizing that having everything he ever dreamed of showed him "that's not the answer" to enduring happiness. His words echo a truth many learn the hard way: reaching the finish line doesn't magically complete the human journey. In fact, neuroscientists find that the chase itself – the striving fueled by dopamine – is what delivers excitement and meaning; once the goal is attained, the brain's reward chemistry recedes, often causing an emotional crash. The result can be a form of the classic "arrival fallacy," a term coined by Tal Ben-Shahar to describe how we mistakenly believe reaching a goal will bring permanent bliss, only to discover that the satisfaction is fleeting. Real-world examples abound. Astronaut Buzz Aldrin, after the historic moon landing, slipped into depression when he returned to Earth and everyday life. He later wrote that after such a pinnacle, *"I wanted to resume my duties, but there were no duties to resume… There was no goal, no sense of calling, no project worth pouring myself into."* His poignant admission of *"no goal"* and *"no sense of calling"* captures the essence of the success void. Achievers may mourn the end of an endeavor because it also means the end of a clear purpose that got them out of bed each day. Until they discover a new mission or redefine their identity in broader terms, a palpable emptiness can shadow even their proudest victories.

Story – The Olympian at the Mountaintop

A powerful illustration of post-achievement identity crisis comes from Olympic legend Michael Phelps. At the height of his success – after winning six gold medals at the 2004 Athens Olympics – Phelps experienced a profound low. He described standing metaphorically "at the top of the mountain" of his life-long dream and thinking: *"[You] work so hard for four years to get to that point, and then it's like you're… at the top of the mountain, you're like what the hell am I supposed to do? Where am I supposed to go? Who am I?".* Here was the most decorated Olympian in history, suddenly unsure of his direction and even his identity once his goal was in hand. Phelps later admitted this was the first time he felt post-Olympic depression – a wave of despondency and aimlessness after the adrenaline of competition subsided. Rather than basking in fulfillment, he was confronted with that unsettling void: *Who am I, beyond the pool?* His identity had been so wrapped up in being a swimmer that once the games were over, he struggled to find footing. Phelps tried to push past these feelings by quickly setting new training goals (he went on to compete in 2008 and 2012), essentially postponing the identity reckoning. But the underlying crisis lingered. "I kind of compartmentalized those feelings and sure enough over time, they decided to reappear whenever they wanted," he said, describing how the unresolved questions about himself kept resurfacing. Eventually, after a DUI arrest and hitting an emotional rock bottom in 2014, Phelps sought therapy and began to confront the core issue: he needed to find an identity beyond "Olympic swimmer." In therapy, he learned to see himself as a person with inherent worth, not solely as an athlete defined by medals. *"I think for a long time I looked at myself as a swimmer and not a human,"* Phelps reflected, recognizing how narrowly he had defined himself. This realization was the turning point. By unpacking "all the extra crap" he had inside and exploring who he was outside of swimming, he started to rebuild his identity on a sturdier foundation. The transformation wasn't overnight – he acknowledges that managing his mental health and sense of self is an ongoing journey. But Phelps emerged with a healthier perspective: he is *more than* his achievements. Today, he channels his energy into new roles – as a mental health advocate, father, and businessman – proving that life after the summit can indeed be rich and meaningful. His story reassures us that questioning one's identity after a major success is normal – it happened even to an Olympian at the very top – and, more importantly, that identity can be rediscovered and renewed beyond the gold medals and titles. Michael Phelps went from wondering if his life had purpose post-Olympics to understanding that being a champion was just one part of him. In the same way, anyone confronting the *"success void"* can take heart that they are more than the trophy they've earned. The titles, awards, and achievements may illuminate one chapter of life, but they do not define the whole story of who you are. By gradually untangling your sense of self from your past accomplishments and exploring new sources of meaning, you can fill that vacuum with a renewed purpose – one that acknowledges you (the person) beyond what you've achieved. Each ending can become a beginning, an opportunity to redefine success on your own terms and continue growing into a fuller identity beyond the summit you've already conquered.

Chapter 4

After the Peak – The Pressure of "What's Next?"

Achieving a major goal is supposed to feel like reaching the summit of a mountain – a moment of triumph and joy. And it often does, briefly. But many high achievers are surprised to find that after the peak experience, a strange void can set in. Psychologists even recognize post-achievement depression: a slump marked by emptiness, restlessness, or lack of purpose following a big accomplishment. This isn't a rare quirk of a few people; it's a shared human experience that can strike anyone from students and writers to athletes and entrepreneurs. Paradoxically, "making it" can leave you feeling unmade – unsure who you are without the climb. In this chapter, we'll explore why success can cast a long shadow and how the question *"What's next?"* can stir up as much anxiety as excitement.

Living in Your Own Shadow

Success can become a double-edged sword. After a personal record or career high, many achievers find themselves living in the shadow of their own past triumph. The very accomplishment that should bring confidence instead sets a daunting benchmark. You might feel that anything less than *outdoing yourself* will be a disappointment. In a sense, you become haunted by the fear of being a "one-hit wonder" in your own life – as if your greatest success might also be your last. This pressure isn't just metaphorical; it's palpable. One entrepreneur described it as the *"second album syndrome"* – wondering if you can repeat the success or if you'll freeze, forever clinging to that one big hit.

Even the legends have felt this fear. After *To Kill a Mockingbird* became an American classic, author Harper Lee never published another novel for 55 years. She admitted, *"Success has had a very bad effect on me… I'm running just as scared as before".* Decades later, in an interview, Lee explained her reluctance: *"When you are at the top, there is only one way to go".* That striking statement reveals the mindset of someone terrified of tarnishing a legacy. If you've reached "the top" (whether that's a bestselling book, a record quarter, or a gold medal performance), it's easy to become *paralyzed by the thought of going downhill.* Instead of basking in success, high achievers often find themselves anxiously asking: *What if that was the peak? What if I never match it again?*

This fear can create a kind of self-imposed shadow that's hard to step out of. Psychologists note that extremely successful, Type-A personalities can be at greater risk for depression, partly due to the loneliness and pressure that accompany big success. It's ironic – the higher you climb, the heavier the pressure not to fall. Public figures like entrepreneurs or artists sometimes admit that external accolades only increase their internal doubts. For example, even Elon Musk – one of the most celebrated innovators – has friends who worry about him, and he has expressed pessimism about his own happiness despite his success. The lesson is that no one is immune to "living in their own shadow." You don't have to be world-famous to feel it. You might be the star sales manager who broke all company records last year, now secretly panicking that you'll never repeat that feat. You might be a community leader who pulled off a hugely successful event, now hesitant to attempt another for fear it won't measure up. In all these cases, success starts to feel less like a victory lap and more like a specter looming behind you, reminding you of a height you're not confident you can reach again.

So why do we do this to ourselves? Part of it is our natural drive and pride. When you achieve something significant, it often becomes a cornerstone of your identity – *I am the person who did X*. That can be motivating, but it can also be trapping. You might feel that to deserve that identity, you must keep proving yourself over and over. Confidence can become oddly fragile after a big win; as one observer noted, *"Nobody was looking the first time around. And now it feels like everyone is waiting for you to fail."*. High achievers can become *hyper-aware* of expectations (both external and internal). Each future attempt carries the weight of "what came before." The shadow of your last success follows you into every boardroom, blank page, or starting block.

Importantly, this mindset isn't permanent or insurmountable – but in the period right after a peak, it can be intense. Recognizing it is the first step. It helps to remember that feeling pressure after success is *incredibly common*. Far from being a sign that something's wrong with you, it's almost a natural byproduct of accomplishment. In fact, many creative and accomplished people have quietly struggled with this "shadow" sensation. They eventually learn that the answer is not to outshine the shadow by sheer force every time – but to step aside and redefine the light. We'll delve into ways to do that in later chapters. For now, it's enough to acknowledge this truth: sometimes the hardest act to follow is your own.

Anxiety of the Blank Page

After the celebrations die down and the congratulations taper off, achievers are often left facing a blank page called the future. This blank page – the open question of "What now?" – can be surprisingly anxiety-inducing. You've been *laser-focused* on a goal for so long that, once it's behind you, an unsettling thought creeps in: *I have no next mission.* While everyone else sees a champion or a success story, you might wake up the next day feeling strangely aimless. Without a new mountain to climb, you feel a restless void.

This phenomenon is widely observed. Olympic athletes, for example, frequently report a psychological crash after the Olympics. They spend years pushing toward one pinnacle. When it's over, many feel a loss of direction. In fact, a University of Toronto study found that nearly a quarter (24%) of Olympians and Paralympians surveyed experienced significant psychological distress in the months after the Games. The end of competition often brings a *"perceived loss of goals and identity,"* especially for those retiring from sport. As one sports psychologist put it, all the hype and intensity drops off quickly after a big event, leaving athletes suddenly asking themselves tough questions: *Do I keep going? Do I find a new path? Who am I if I stop?.* These questions can be even more anxiety-inducing than the competition itself, because they strike at the core of a person's identity and purpose.

And it's not just Olympians. Consider legendary astronaut Buzz Aldrin, who walked on the Moon in 1969. After that literal peak experience, Aldrin struggled profoundly with what came next. He realized there was *"no goal, no sense of calling, no project worth pouring myself into"* once the moon mission was over. He described coming back to Earth (both physically and emotionally) as confronting *"magnificent desolation"* – an overwhelming emptiness despite the magnitude of his achievement. With no idea how to top the moon landing, Aldrin fell into depression and drifted aimlessly for a time, feeling he was "heading into an abyss" of purposelessness. His story may be dramatic, but the underlying dynamic is universal: when you finish writing one epic chapter of your life, the blank page of the next chapter can provoke deep anxiety.

Why does an *open future* cause such unease? One reason is that ambitious people are used to having a target. The structure and striving of working toward a goal can keep anxiety at bay – it's clear what you need to do when you're on a mission. Once the mission is accomplished, there's a sudden *absence of direction*. High achievers often tie their energy and even self-worth to pursuing something. Without a plan or purpose, you might feel "rudderless," as mental health experts describe it. There's an internal pressure that says, *"I should be doing something important… but what?"* Idle time that others might find relaxing can make an achiever feel uneasy or guilty.

Additionally, there's the fear of choosing the "wrong" next goal. With a blank page, theoretically *anything* is possible – and that paradox of choice can be paralyzing. After one success, you might feel your next move is critical, so it'd better be good. This all-or-nothing thinking ramps up anxiety. It's as if you're standing at a crossroads with countless paths, unsure which one leads to another fulfilling summit and which might be a dead end.

Michael Phelps, the most decorated Olympian, captured this feeling well. After his record-breaking Olympic victories, Phelps said he experienced a post-Olympic depression and found himself wondering, *"You're at the top of the mountain... what the hell am I supposed to do? Where am I supposed to go? Who am I?"*. That stark trio of questions – *What do I do? Where do I go? Who am I?* – reveals how success can unsettle even our sense of identity. When your life has been structured around a huge goal, achieving it can leave you questioning everything from your daily routine to your broader purpose.

It's important to recognize that this blank-page anxiety is not a sign of weakness or ingratitude for your success. It's a natural emotional response to the end of a long journey. The drive that fueled you up the mountain runs out of fuel at the summit – and it takes time to refuel and reorient. In these moments, many achievers actually discover that happiness was more tied to the process than the outcome. The chase, the climb, the *purpose* is what gave them energy. So when that's gone, a kind of emotional hangover sets in. Psychologists call this the "arrival fallacy," the mistaken belief that once you reach your goal you'll be happy forever.

In reality, humans adapt quickly to accomplishments, and our happiness tends to fall back to baseline once the novelty wears off. The goal achieved doesn't sustain us; it's often the pursuit that gave us meaning.

So if you find yourself anxious or blue after a big win, remember: it's common and it's chemical. Part of it is literally your biology coming off a high. During the pursuit, your brain was releasing dopamine – the "achievement hormone" – to keep you focused and motivated. When you finally hold the prize, that dopamine rush subsides, making it *biochemically more challenging to feel happy* in the immediate aftermath. Knowing this can help you be gentle with yourself. Your brain and heart are simply recalibrating to a new reality. The blank page *will* eventually get filled – with new goals, new passions or new definitions of success – but it's okay to stare at it uncertainly for a while. In later chapters we'll discuss how to find direction and purpose again. For now, give yourself permission to feel a little lost. Sometimes, standing at sea level after a summit can feel disorienting – but it also means a new journey can begin when you're ready.

No Rest for the Winner

After achieving something great, you might imagine you'd kick back in a well-earned rest. In reality, many achievers find it *incredibly hard to relax and savor their success*. Instead of a victory lap, there's a nagging voice saying: *Keep pushing.* People in this mindset often report a mix of fatigue and urgency – they're tired from the last climb, yet already feeling pressure to start scaling the next peak. The irony is thick: you achieve a goal, and it actually *robs* you of the freedom to rest (at least it feels that way). Why does this happen?

One reason is the fear of losing momentum. When you've been operating at full throttle, slowing down can feel dangerous. High performers worry that if they stop to rest, they'll fall behind or "lose their edge." In workplaces and competitive fields, there's a common saying that *"you're only as good as your last success."* That cultural pressure seeps into the achiever's psyche. You may think, *If I pause now, will I ever get back to this level?* or *Everyone's expecting me to continue at this high level – I can't let up.* This creates a scenario where winners don't feel they have permission to celebrate or recuperate. Anecdotally, some startup founders who sell their companies for millions are back at it with a new venture almost immediately – not necessarily because they need more money, but because they feel they *should* keep producing big things.

Another factor is identity and habit. Driven individuals often thrive on the chase (as we saw with dopamine and motivation). Once the goal is done, they miss the structure and excitement of pursuit. There's almost an addictive element: the rush of accomplishment fades, and they crave the next win to feel that high again. This can lead to a *"never enough"* cycle where no achievement ever feels final. Instead of enjoying the view from the summit, the achiever's gaze instantly shifts to finding a taller mountain.

Society reinforces this, too. We live in a culture that celebrates productivity and constant striving. The messages are everywhere: *What's your next project? How will you top that? Don't rest on your laurels!* While ambition can be positive, relentless striving with no respite is a recipe for burnout. It's telling that burnout is often highest among high achievers in demanding fields – people who achieved a lot but at the cost of chronic stress. High achievers can internalize the idea that taking a break equals being lazy or unworthy. Some even feel *guilty* for wanting downtime, as if success is a burden they must carry without setting it down. They may recall nights or weekends they "lost" to working toward the goal and feel they must continue that level of sacrifice to maintain their status.

However, this *"no rest for the winner"* mentality is as unsustainable as it is common. Our bodies and minds are not machines, and even machines need maintenance. Interestingly, even at the elite level, we see a shift: many coaches and psychologists now emphasize recovery as part of high performance. Olympic athletes, for example, are encouraged to take time off after major events to recharge – because not doing so can lead to physical injury and mental breakdown. One two-time Olympic gold medalist, soccer player Briana Scurry, explicitly advises new champions to plan a post-achievement break, whether it's a vacation or a simple change of pace, because rest is crucial for long-term success. In her words, "At the end of the day, the Olympics part of your life will end… You have a lot of time for the other parts". That is a healthy reminder that life is bigger than any one accomplishment, and taking care of yourself ensures you can enjoy *all* parts of life.

Yet for the person in the moment, such advice can be hard to heed. If you're feeling that *twitch* to immediately do more, try to step back and ask: Who am I trying to impress or reassure? Often, achievers keep pushing not because they truly want to at that moment, but because they feel they *have to* in order to maintain an image – either in others' eyes or their own. Recognizing this pressure is the first step to releasing it. Success should ideally grant you *more* freedom, not less. If you can grant yourself permission, take that victory lap – literally or figuratively. Celebrate the win, reflect on the journey, and allow a pause. It might feel uncomfortable at first, but rest is not the enemy of success; it is the fuel for future success. In fact, chronic overdrive can dull the creativity and passion that make achievements meaningful. Just as fields need fallow seasons and athletes need off-seasons, your mind and drive need rest to rejuvenate. Otherwise, you risk turning a joyous accomplishment into the starting point of burnout.

It's worth noting that burnout after success is a documented phenomenon. When high achievers don't pause, they can hit a wall emotionally. They might suddenly lose motivation or feel empty despite outward success. This is the mind and body's way of enforcing a break that wasn't willingly taken. Avoiding rest is like ignoring a finish line and forcing yourself to keep running – eventually, you collapse. So, as hard as it might be, *taking a break is part of the process of sustained achievement.* True champions learn to balance effort with recovery. You haven't "gone soft" by enjoying your success; you're recharging for whatever comes next, on your own terms.

Story – The Second Album Syndrome

To illustrate these post-peak pressures, let's look at a story that might feel familiar. Meet Julie, a novelist who experienced a meteoric rise – and

41

then the weight of "what's next" nearly crushed her spirit. Julie spent years quietly writing a novel in her free time. She poured her heart into it, not knowing if it would ever see the light of day. Eventually, her manuscript was picked up by a publisher, and in a twist of fate, her debut novel became a blockbuster hit. Critics hailed it as a masterpiece; it hit bestseller lists and even got optioned for a movie. Overnight, Julie went from an unknown writer to "the next big thing" in literature.

At first, Julie was overjoyed. This was the summit of the mountain she had dreamed of climbing. But as the months passed, the glow of success began to dim. In its place came an unexpected dread. When she sat down at her desk to start her next book, she was confronted with a blank page – and for the first time in her life, writer's block. Not the mild, temporary kind, but a deep paralysis. Every time Julie tried to write, a voice in her head taunted: *What if this isn't as good as the last one?* She felt like she was *living in the shadow of her own novel.* The world was watching now; readers were waiting eagerly for her follow-up. Instead of writing freely like she used to, she found herself agonizing over every sentence, comparing it to her previous work. She'd type a line, then delete it, convinced it wasn't brilliant enough. Days turned into weeks, and Julie's anxiety grew. She confided to a friend, *"I'm terrified of being a one-hit wonder. What if I only had that one story in me?"*

Julie's fear was not just about the book; it was about her identity. Before, she was an unknown aspiring writer – no pressure, nothing to lose. Now she was "Julie, the best-selling author," and she felt she had *everything to lose.* People would say, *"I can't wait to see if she tops the first book!"*

To Julie, these innocent comments felt like immense pressure. She began to avoid writing altogether. Her once-beloved morning routine of jotting down ideas over coffee became a time of dread. She'd do anything else – clean the house, scroll her phone – to escape facing that blank page. The joy had been sucked out of the creative process, replaced by performance anxiety.

This is a classic case of Second Album Syndrome. In the music world, artists who have a smash debut often struggle with their sophomore album, fearing they can't replicate the magic. Julie was experiencing the writer's version. In fact, one famous singer, Dusty Springfield, delayed her second album for years because she was so afraid it wouldn't live up to her first. Julie felt a kinship with that story now. She even found solace reading about authors like Harper Lee, who chose not to publish again for decades. It reassured her that she wasn't simply being "weak" or ungrateful – success really can be daunting. As one article she read put it, *it's tough to feel pinned beneath the boulder of your own reputation, worrying that nothing will ever be as good.*

Meanwhile, on the other side of the country, an entrepreneur named Tom was facing his own post-peak crisis. Tom had co-founded a tech startup in his twenties, and after years of grind, he struck gold – a larger company acquired his startup in a multi-million-dollar deal. It was the dream outcome. Colleagues and friends congratulated him heartily, and the tech press wrote headlines like *"Young Founder's Big Win – What Will He Do Next?"* At first, Tom was ecstatic (and a bit relieved) to have "made it." But very quickly, that question – *"What's next?"* – stopped being fun and started keeping him up at night.

With a sudden windfall and no immediate job, Tom felt unmoored. Like Julie, he woke up with a blank page in front of him. But instead of enjoying some downtime, he felt *restless*. In Silicon Valley culture, the expectation is often that a successful founder will become a "serial entrepreneur" – either starting a new company right away or becoming an investor and mentor. Tom could sense the unspoken pressure: *Don't just sit around, you need to create the next big thing.* At networking events, people would ask, *"Have you got another startup in the works?"* He smiled and gave vague answers, but internally Tom was anxious. What if my last success was a fluke? He wondered if he had gotten lucky and if he really had the talent to do it again. The thought of starting from scratch on a new venture felt daunting – the tech world would expect greatness from him now. He even hesitated to advise other startups despite his experience, thinking, *If my next thing fails, I'll look like a fraud for giving advice.*

Tom's predicament was essentially the entrepreneurial version of Second Album Syndrome. He was a hero of one story, now petrified about the sequel. At first, he threw himself into busywork – taking meetings, dabbling in side projects – unable to just *rest on his laurels*. In quiet moments, he admitted to himself that he missed the hustle of building something, yet he was also bone-tired from years of overwork. Still, he felt guilty even considering a sabbatical. Whenever he tried to take it easy, a voice in his head accused him of wasting time and potential.

Both Julie and Tom illustrate how success can become a source of stress. For Julie, the creative joy was replaced by pressure to live up to her own success. For Tom, the triumph of a big win was followed by an identity crisis and fear of not measuring up in his next chapter. Their stories may differ in details, but they share a key theme: after reaching a summit, the next steps can feel overwhelmingly uncertain and heavy.

Now, how did their stories progress? Julie, after months of struggle, finally had a breakthrough – not in writing, but in mindset. In frustration one day, she decided, *"Forget it, I'm just going to write something for fun, even if it's terrible."* She gave herself permission to *play* with words again, as if no one would ever read them. Slowly, this loosened the creative knots. She wrote a short story that wasn't meant to be her "next big novel," just a story to enjoy. That act rekindled her love of writing without the pressure. Eventually, Julie started a second novel, deliberately trying a different genre and style so she wouldn't be constantly comparing it to her first book. She told herself, *maybe it won't be a bestseller, but it will be my next mountain to climb, and that's what I need.* Bit by bit, the shadow of her first success started to shrink as she stepped out of it on her own terms.

Tom's turning point came when an older mentor bluntly told him, *"You've got nothing to prove. The fact that you built something great once doesn't mean you owe the world another – do it only if you want to."* This resonated. Tom realized he had been *chasing others' approval* rather than his own passion. He took an unexpected route: he decided to join a nonprofit's board and advise a young social enterprise for a while, just to engage in meaningful work without the pressure of being the guy in charge. During this period, he rediscovered the parts of entrepreneurship he loved – creativity, problem-solving, teamwork – without the weight of expectation. Ironically, by stepping back, he eventually felt the genuine spark of a new idea he *wanted* to pursue, rather than one he felt *obligated* to pursue.

The experiences of Julie and Tom show that the "What's next?" pressure, as intimidating as it is, can be managed and overcome. The key insight is that they both had to reframe how they viewed success and their identity. They learned that you are more than your last achievement. Julie came to see herself not just as "the author of *that* famous novel," but as a writer who has a whole creative life ahead – allowed to have ups and downs. Tom realized he didn't have to start the next billion-dollar company right away to be a "real" entrepreneur; he could contribute value in smaller ways until he found a venture that truly inspired him.

In the end, both took the bold step of defining their next chapter on their own terms, rather than letting the shadow of the previous one dictate it. That's a lesson any milestone achiever can take to heart. The pressure of "What's next?" may never fully disappear – there will always be some uncertainty in life after a peak. But by acknowledging the pressure, understanding where it comes from, and giving yourself space to breathe and grow, you can turn that blank page from a source of anxiety into a canvas of possibility. The next summit might not be taller, but it can be more meaningful. And above all, you'll discover that life after the summit is still rich with purpose – if you have the courage to seek it beyond the glory of yesterday.

Chapter 5

The Hidden Toll of Triumph –
Burnout, Isolation, and Emotional
Fallout

A chieving a long-sought goal is often imagined as a moment of pure joy and lasting fulfillment. Yet many high achievers discover a more complicated reality once the celebrations fade. The hidden toll of triumph can include exhaustion, loneliness, and unexpected emotional struggles that lurk behind the outward glory of success. It turns out that reaching the summit – whether it's a career milestone, a personal best, or a lifelong dream – can leave a person feeling drained, isolated, or even disillusioned rather than perpetually ecstatic. This chapter pulls back the curtain on that paradox. It explores how *burnout* can hit right after victory, why it can feel "lonely at the top," how guilt often accompanies post-success sadness, and why openly acknowledging these feelings is so important. By understanding these hidden costs of achievement, readers will see that they are not alone – and that feeling a void after "making it" is a human experience shared by many.

Burnout Behind the Glory

The push to achieve something great often demands everything you have – long hours, intense focus, and a surge of adrenaline powering you through obstacles. But when the finish line is crossed, that same adrenaline subsides and can leave you utterly spent. The period *after* a big win frequently brings a physical and mental crash. In fact, psychologists note that post-achievement feelings of *"lack of motivation" and "tiredness"* are common once a long-standing goal is completed. This isn't due to laziness or weakness – it's the understandable result of the enormous effort it took to succeed. Your body and mind, revved at full throttle for so long, are now desperately trying to recover.

Figure: The Olympic rings at sunset symbolize the end of a journey – even triumphant athletes often face a psychological comedown after the Games. The "post-Olympic blues" are well documented: athletes describe coming down from an adrenaline-fueled high and feeling empty or listless once the competition is over. The intense high of the event is followed by a notable low as hormone levels and excitement plummet. This dynamic illustrates that even the ultimate victories have a hidden cost. After the thrill of victory wears off, athletes and non-athletes alike can experience a period of profound fatigue and mood decline. What looks like the pinnacle of glory from the outside can mask an exhausted mind and body recalibrating to normal life.

In everyday terms, it's like running your car at top speed and then suddenly slamming the brakes – the engine sputters and needs time to cool down. High achievers often report that in the days or weeks after a major accomplishment, they feel physically fatigued, emotionally depleted, and purposeless, sometimes called the "post-event blues." Medical experts note that this crash can leave you *"sad, listless, empty or questioning your purpose in life"* once the adrenaline fades. The body's stress response, which kept you going through the final stretch, now subsides, and with it goes the energy and excitement that were propping you up. It's no wonder that someone who was running on all cylinders might suddenly find themselves barely able to get out of bed after the big day.

Consider the story of media mogul Arianna Huffington – outwardly one of the most successful, driven people in the world. In 2007, not long after scaling her own summit with the growth of *The Huffington Post*, she collapsed from exhaustion. She woke up on the floor with a broken cheekbone, having pushed herself beyond the limit. *"Outwardly, she was the picture of success,"* a profile noted, yet as she underwent medical tests she began to wonder, *"Is this really what success feels like?"*. Huffington's wake-up call revealed the burnout behind the glory – the way extraordinary effort can take a severe toll on health. Her experience isn't an isolated case of one overworked CEO; it exemplifies a pattern seen in many fields. People who pour heart and soul into reaching a goal may ignore mounting fatigue or stress injuries (physical and mental) until *after* the finish, when the body finally forces a reckoning.

This "burnout behind the glory" can manifest as more than just needing a nap. Some newly-minted graduates, for example, spend their final semester in a sleepless sprint to finish a thesis or earn honors – only to come home after graduation and feel unable to focus or motivate themselves for weeks. New founders might drive a startup to a successful launch and then hit an energy wall, finding themselves strangely apathetic or ill once the immediate pressure lifts. The phenomenon even has a biological angle: during the *chase* for a goal, the brain rewards us with dopamine and other stress hormones that keep us alert and energized. But once the goal is attained, those neurochemical levels drop sharply, contributing to feelings of emptiness or deflation. In other words, the very chemistry that made the journey exhilarating also guarantees that the end of the journey will feel like hitting a void.

Another vivid example comes from the world of sports. Olympic athletes often spend years in intense training, their lives oriented around a single competition. After the Olympics, many report an emotional hangover so common that it's been dubbed the "Olympic comedown." Sport psychologists compare it to withdrawal from a drug – the "high" of competition stems in part from a flood of adrenaline, and when it's over, the sudden absence of that rush can lead to a depressive slump. One Olympic medalist, British runner Keely Hodgkinson, admitted she was caught off guard by how low she felt after her success. In her words, *"I didn't realize Olympic comedown was actually a big thing,"* acknowledging that after the adrenaline of winning silver at the Tokyo Games, she fell into a depression. If even an elite athlete standing on the podium can feel *drained and blue* following victory, it underscores a powerful lesson: post-achievement burnout is real, and it doesn't mean something is wrong with you. It means you've been through a period of intense output, and your system is recalibrating.

Understanding this dynamic reassures us that feeling *spent* or unmotivated after a win is not a character flaw. It's a natural response to an extraordinary effort. Psychologists have even given a name to the mistaken expectation that reaching a goal will bring endless happiness –

the "arrival fallacy," coined by Tal Ben-Shahar. We might fantasize that finishing the marathon, getting the promotion, or publishing the book will put us on a permanent high. In reality, as countless achievers learn, the human mind quickly adjusts. The intense focus of the journey is replaced by a kind of void, and the body that was running on adrenaline may demand rest in the form of fatigue or burnout. The key takeaway is that post-achievement fatigue is common and temporary. It calls for recovery: just as muscles need to heal after climbing a mountain, your mental and emotional "muscles" need downtime after an all-out push. Far from being laziness, this downtime is a necessary healing phase, and respecting it can prevent a temporary slump from deepening into chronic burnout.

Alone at the Top

Another hidden toll of triumph is isolation. There's a saying: *"It's lonely at the top."* While it sounds cliché, many people who reach a pinnacle find an unexpected loneliness awaiting them. You might assume that after a big achievement, you'll be basking in congratulations and camaraderie. And indeed, accolades do come – but they often come with an assumption that you're *on cloud nine* and have no reason to feel anything but happy. Meanwhile, you might be wrestling with complex feelings that people around you don't understand. Who can you confide in when it seems like you have it all? High achievers often feel that they've lost the right to complain, and this pressure to "always be okay" can create a profound sense of alienation.

One reason for feeling alone at the top is that success can set you apart from your peers. If you were part of a close-knit group and suddenly rise to a position of greater success (say, a promotion to an executive role above your friends, or winning a championship that others only dream of), the social dynamic shifts. You may sense envy from some, or just a lack of relatable feedback – after all, few people around you have experienced the pressures you have. A study in the *Journal of Leadership & Organizational Studies* found that senior managers and executives tend to be lonelier both at work and outside of work than those at lower levels, largely because of the demands and unique pressures of their roles. CEOs in particular often have no true peers at the office – they sit at the top of the hierarchy and can't freely chat about their insecurities or stresses with subordinates. The higher you climb, the fewer people there are who *really* understand what your days look like or how heavy your crown feels.

Even when friends or family try to be supportive, a successful person can feel a distance open up. Imagine a scenario: you poured everything into launching your small business and it became a hit. Your friends still care about you, but they might make offhand comments like, "Well, you did it – you're set for life now!" They're proud of you, yet such comments might make you feel unable to voice any struggles. If you mention stress or exhaustion, you might get puzzled looks or even dismissal: "What do *you* have to be stressed about? You've succeeded!" This dynamic silences many achievers. They put on a smile and say "I'm fine," all the while feeling nobody to talk to about the confusion or loneliness they actually feel. As one executive described it, success can create an *"absence of being truly seen"* by others – you are surrounded by people, yet feel that no one grasps your inner reality.

The isolation is not just emotional; it can also be practical. When you're at the top, whether that's in an organization or in your personal milestone, you often have fewer people you can confide in without repercussions. Leaders worry about burdening their team or appearing vulnerable. A revealing survey of CEOs found that half of them experience feelings of loneliness in their career, and of those, a majority (61%) believe that loneliness hinders their performance. It's telling that even at the very top of business, where one might assume people are surrounded by advisors and admirers, *many leaders quietly feel alone.* This loneliness isn't just an inconvenience; it can become a serious issue, affecting decision-making and well-being. When you feel you must *bear every burden alone*, stress multiplies. It's hard to know where to turn when everyone assumes you're confidently enjoying your success.

Success often creates a gap between high achievers and those around them. Colleagues might treat a newly promoted leader differently, and old friends might struggle to relate to a suddenly "famous" peer. The higher one climbs, the fewer people there are who share similar experiences, which can intensify feelings of isolation. This image of a person alone in a high office highlights how triumph can separate someone from the crowd, at least in their own perception. The loneliness is not always visible from the outside; to others, the person "up there" looks powerful and self-sufficient. But inside, they may feel like they're on an island.

Another aspect of post-achievement isolation is the sense that others don't want to hear about your problems – because your life looks enviable. This can particularly affect people whose success thrusts them into the public eye or a vastly different lifestyle. For instance, new celebrities or public figures often struggle with this. They might be dealing with relentless pressure or anxiety, but expressing it is hard when any complaint invites backlash like, "Celebrities have nothing to be depressed about with all that money and fame." Such attitudes force achievers to bottle up their struggles, deepening the sense of aloneness. Even among friends, a successful person might hesitate to share their worries about, say, managing newfound wealth or the strain of constant high performance, because it can sound like bragging or ungratefulness. Consequently, they bear the emotional weight in silence.

Importantly, feeling alone at the top does *not* mean you actually have no allies or friends. Often, it's the perception and pressure that create isolation. People think you're celebrating, so they give you space – perhaps too much space. Or they assume you wouldn't want to hear about their mundane problems now. Ironically, both sides withdraw: the achiever doesn't reach out because they assume others won't understand, and others don't check in because they assume the achiever is doing great. This mutual miscommunication can leave successful individuals in a kind of celebratory quarantine: everyone cheers them on from a distance, but few engage with their real emotional state. If you've felt this way, know that it's not unusual. The challenge is finding ways to bridge that gap – by gently letting trusted people know that *having success doesn't mean you're invulnerable.* In the next section, we'll delve into one big reason people hesitate to admit they're struggling after a win: the guilt and shame that can accompany post-success sadness.

The Guilt of Discontent

Perhaps one of the cruelest facets of post-achievement depression is the guilt that often tags along with it. You've achieved what you set out to do – shouldn't you be grateful and happy? Many people ask themselves this question with a heavy heart, wondering *"What's wrong with me?"* when they don't feel on top of the world after a success. Society certainly reinforces the idea that we ought to be *nothing but joyful* when we've "made it." As a result, feeling unhappy or empty after an accomplishment can trigger a sense of shame or self-judgment. Instead of recognizing post-goal blues as a normal come-down, high achievers often berate themselves for it, thinking they're being ungrateful or "spoiled." This section addresses that internal conflict: why you might hide your disappointment behind a forced smile, and why feeling discontent despite success is nothing to be ashamed of.

A major source of this guilt is the narrative we carry about success and happiness. We're often taught that reaching our goals is the key to fulfillment – a message so pervasive that Tal Ben-Shahar labeled it the *arrival fallacy*, the false belief that achieving a particular goal will deliver lasting happiness. We chase the promotion, the gold medal, the published novel with the sincere idea that life will be *better* and we'll be satisfied at the summit. So when reality sets in and we experience sadness, boredom, or lack of purpose after the initial victory, it completely contradicts our expectations. There's a gap between how we *thought* we'd feel and how we actually feel. As one analysis put it, we often set lofty expectations for how ecstatic we'll be after a major accomplishment, and if the reality doesn't measure up, disillusionment hits hard. Instead of the permanent high we anticipated, we may find that everyday life creeps back in, or new challenges quickly replace the old ones. This expectation-reality gap can lead to an internal narrative that *"I must be doing something wrong if I'm not happy now."*

That's where guilt seeps in. Achievers might think about all the people who supported them, or those who *haven't* achieved the same thing, and feel guilty for not reveling in success 24/7. "How dare I be dissatisfied," the thinking goes, "when others would kill to be in my shoes?" One coach described how high performers can end up *"feeling half-hearted about every part of our lives, no matter how successful or abundant they may seem from the outside."* That half-heartedness often shows up as worry, self-doubt, rumination, and guilt — specifically, *guilt for not feeling happy, despite how hard we worked to achieve everything we thought would finally and fully satisfy us.* In other words, you might have checked all the boxes and done everything "right," yet your emotions didn't get the memo. The resulting discontent feels illegitimate. Instead of treating it as a signal that something needs attention (be it rest, meaning, or connection), people berate themselves for ingratitude.

This guilt of discontent can be exacerbated by external voices as well. Well-meaning friends or family might say things like, "Come on, you should be proud!" or "I wish I had your problems!" if you hint at not being happy. Such responses, even if intended to cheer you up, often have the opposite effect: they reinforce the feeling that *you're not allowed to feel bad.* Consequently, many achievers learn to put on a mask of positivity. They go through the motions of celebration, post the obligatory happy photos on social media, and say all the right things about how thankful they are. Inside, though, they may feel like frauds for doing so, further feeding the cycle of guilt. It becomes a private torment: *feeling unhappy →* *feeling guilty for being unhappy → feeling even more unhappy because of the guilt.* This loop can spiral, sometimes leading people to hide their feelings even deeper, which unfortunately also delays seeking help or finding a path forward.

It's critical to break that cycle by recognizing a fundamental truth: achieving something major doesn't flip a magic switch that makes you immune to unhappiness. Human emotions are complex and not bound to our résumés or trophy cases. You can be profoundly appreciative of the opportunities you've had and the people who helped you, and simultaneously feel lost or down. These emotions are not mutually exclusive, nor does sadness after success erase the value of the achievement. It helps to realize that a form of *grief* often accompanies the end of a journey – you are, in a sense, mourning the conclusion of a meaningful pursuit, or the loss of a guiding purpose that drove you. Feeling a bit empty after that is natural. Gratitude and grief can coexist. You can be grateful for your success and still acknowledge that you're struggling emotionally. There is no need for shame in that.

Moreover, feeling discontent does not mean you're an ungrateful person; it means you're a person, *period.* Emotions don't always line up neatly with circumstances. Plenty of lottery winners, for example, have experienced depression or a loss of direction after the initial high – not because money is bad, but because suddenly one chapter of striving ended and a big question ("What now?") loomed. The mind needs purpose and challenge; when one goal is over, it often takes time to reorient to the next, and during that transition, malaise can settle in. High achievers are used to striving. When the strive is over, it's common to feel uneasy or even guilty for *not striving*. Recognize that this is a transitional phase. It doesn't make you unworthy of your success or undeserving of sympathy. In fact, acknowledging the disconnect between outer success and inner feelings is the first step to addressing it honestly.

By confronting the guilt head-on, you start to *loosen its power*. Try reframing your internal dialogue: instead of "I shouldn't feel this way," gently remind yourself why you might feel this way (exhaustion, lost routine, the big expectation build-up). Remember that others have felt the same. You are not the only one to wonder why happiness didn't automatically arrive with the trophy. There are documented cases of highly accomplished individuals – from famous actors to entrepreneurs – who fell into funks or depression after their big wins. They, too, initially felt guilt or confusion about it. The turning point often comes when they stop judging themselves for feeling that way. By giving yourself permission to feel whatever you feel, you remove one layer of suffering (the self-blame) and can focus on moving forward. The next section will show that more people are beginning to talk about these very struggles, helping to normalize them. It's increasingly clear: feeling unhappy despite success is nothing to be ashamed of, and acknowledging it is a sign of honesty and self-awareness, not ingratitude.

Breaking the Taboo

For a long time, admitting to burnout, loneliness, or depression at the height of success was considered taboo. High achievers were expected to be role models of positivity and strength – any cracks in that façade were often hidden from public view. However, this silence has begun to break. In recent years, a number of renowned individuals have courageously spoken out about their mental health struggles after big wins or during high-profile success, helping to chip away at the stigma. Their message: *It's okay to not be okay, even when things look great on the outside.* By sharing their stories, these figures are encouraging others to acknowledge and voice their own struggles without embarrassment. This cultural shift is vital, because it reframes seeking help as a form of strength rather than weakness.

It's striking to see who is coming forward. Pop superstar Lady Gaga has openly discussed her battles with depression and trauma, despite her global fame and accolades. British royalty Prince Harry has candidly talked about his bouts of anxiety and the benefits of therapy, even though many would assume a prince's life is idyllic. In the business world, media icon Oprah Winfrey and tech leader Elon Musk have alluded to their own mental health challenges, showing that wealth and influence don't make one invulnerable. Even elite athletes, like NHL hockey star Jonathan Toews – a Stanley Cup champion – have shared their struggles with depression. These are people at the pinnacle of diverse fields (entertainment, royalty, business, sports), and their willingness to say "I have struggled" carries enormous weight. It validates the experiences of anyone going through a post-achievement low: if they can have these feelings and still be respected, so can you.

Each time a public figure breaks the silence, it sends a powerful message that mental health issues do not discriminate by success level. The impact of these celebrity disclosures on reducing stigma is even being studied by experts. When a famous person admits "I felt empty after my big accomplishment" or "I dealt with depression even when I was winning," it challenges the norm of concealing such feelings and encourages everyday people to speak up or seek help. As one mental health expert noted, *"When someone in the public eye is open and honest about their mental health, it can have positive outcomes. First, it reduces shame and prejudice that has long kept mental health in the shadows. Second, it encourages people who may have mental illness to seek care."* In other words, these brave admissions create a ripple effect: they normalize the conversation and reassure others that they're not "crazy" or alone for feeling depressed after success.

We're seeing the start of a culture where discussing burnout or depression is not a career-ender or a source of humiliation, but rather seen as an aspect of overall health. In Hollywood, for instance, more actors and filmmakers have spoken about the anxiety and emotional crashes that follow big premieres or award wins. In corporate circles, some CEOs have begun to share their personal mental health journeys in interviews or company memos, encouraging a healthier workplace dialogue. This collective acknowledgement cracks the old facade that *everything is perfect* at the top. It also highlights that getting help – whether through therapy, support groups, or talking to a doctor – is a wise and proactive step. Consider that even the most successful athletes have coaches and trainers for their physical well-being; similarly, tending to mental well-being is just part of staying in shape for life's challenges.

For readers who find themselves in the afterglow (or shadow) of an achievement and are struggling, the takeaway is: you have permission to speak about it. Breaking the taboo might start in a personal way – confiding in a close friend that you're actually having a tough time, or being honest with a mentor about your lack of direction post-success. You might be pleasantly surprised at the response. Often, opening up invites others to share their own similar feelings, and suddenly that wall of isolation begins to crumble. You realize that what you thought was a unique flaw is actually a fairly common human experience. By voicing it, you also give others in your circle *permission* to be honest. It creates a ripple of authenticity that benefits everyone.

It's also important to challenge the narrative in our own minds that admitting struggle equals weakness. In truth, it takes strength and courage to acknowledge when you're not okay, especially in a world that might expect you to be celebrating. There is a shift happening in the definition of strength: from stoically bearing everything alone to responsibly acknowledging when you need support. Just as one would not hesitate to treat a broken leg after a victorious game, we must learn not to hesitate in treating a bout of depression or severe burnout after a victorious life event. Seeking help – through counseling, joining a support community, talking to a doctor about possible therapy or medication – is a proactive and brave action. It demonstrates self-awareness and a commitment to one's well-being. As the public dialogue around these issues grows, hopefully more people will feel safe to take that step without feeling "weak."

In fact, sharing your story, even on a small scale, might help someone else. You don't need to be famous for your experience to matter. Perhaps a colleague is quietly going through a similar post-success void and thinks they're the only one. By opening up about your own challenges, you could become part of breaking the taboo in your community. It creates a support network where previously there was silent suffering. The more we all talk about the hidden toll of triumph, the more we normalize the fact that success and happiness are not one and the same – and that's okay.

In conclusion, this chapter has shown that after the summit, it's not unusual to feel a void. Burnout, isolation, and emotional fallout are real, but they *can* be overcome. By recognizing burnout as a natural recovery phase, by understanding that loneliness can be alleviated through connecting with those who "get it," by forgiving yourself for any discontent, and by speaking openly about mental health, you pave the way for a healthier relationship with achievement. The summit is not the end of your story; it's just one peak, and after it comes a new journey. Armed with openness and self-compassion, you can navigate the success void and rebuild purpose beyond your accomplishments. Remember, it's okay to not feel okay after a big win. What's not okay is suffering in silence or believing you're somehow broken for feeling that way. The hidden toll of triumph becomes far less daunting when we shine a light on it – together.

Chapter 6

Facing the Void – Acceptance as a First Step

Normalizing the Letdown

After the rush of achievement, a surprising emptiness can set in. Imagine an Olympic champion stepping off the podium or an entrepreneur selling their start-up for millions – only to feel strangely hollow the next day. This "down" after the high is more common than you might think. In fact, post-achievement blues are a normal human response. There is nothing wrong with you for experiencing a letdown after success. On the contrary, feeling a come-down after a big high is practically wired into our biology and psychology.

Consider the stories of real high achievers: Michael Phelps, one of the most decorated Olympians ever, has openly discussed how *after* winning gold medals he sank into depression, asking "What now?" Similarly, Buzz Aldrin – one of the first men to walk on the moon – returned to Earth and fell into a deep depression, struggling because nothing in everyday life could compare to that pinnacle moment. These examples might sound extreme, but they illustrate a universal truth: no summit stays euphoric forever. If even astronauts and Olympic champions feel a void after reaching the peak, it underscores that this emotional crash is not a personal failing – it's a human phenomenon.

Why does this happen? Part of the answer lies in our brain chemistry and the nature of pursuit. When you were striving toward your goal, your brain was likely flooded with dopamine – a neurochemical that motivates us and makes us feel good as we make progress. Psychologists point out that during the chase, each small win gave you a little hit of pleasure and excitement. Your days had structure, purpose, and anticipation. But once you finally hit the finish line, that stream of feel-good brain chemicals slows down. The exciting chase is over, and biologically it's harder to feel the same thrill. It's as if your brain's reward engine has idled down, leaving you in a quiet lull.

There's even a name for the disappointment that can follow accomplishment: the "arrival fallacy." Coined by a positive psychology expert, this term means the false belief that once you *arrive* at a goal, you'll achieve lasting happiness. We often imagine that success will be a permanent high – *if I could just get that promotion, win that award, reach that sales target, then I'll be happy forever.* If only it were that simple. In reality, the satisfaction after reaching a milestone is usually temporary. You might feel a brief surge of pride or joy, but then life continues. The mountaintop moment passes, and normalcy resumes – sometimes with an emotional valley in its wake.

It's important to normalize this emotional trajectory. You are not broken or ungrateful for feeling a bit low after a win; you are *human.* Almost anyone who pours their heart into a long-term goal experiences some void when it's done. Graduates often feel a blues after the graduation ceremony is over. Newlyweds can experience a dip in mood after the excitement of a wedding. Authors frequently report a strange sadness after finishing a book manuscript. Athletes, after the big championship, wonder why they aren't on cloud nine indefinitely. This pattern spans all walks of life – from the student who finally earns that degree, to the executive who reaches a career pinnacle, to the traveler returning home from a life-changing adventure.

Understanding that this letdown is *known and expected* can be a huge relief. It means you can stop beating yourself up for "not being happy like I'm supposed to." There is no "supposed to" when it comes to complex emotions. Feeling a post-success void doesn't mean you failed to appreciate your accomplishment; it means the accomplishment mattered to you. Your mind and body are simply recalibrating now that the big push is over. In a sense, this low is the natural counterbalance to the intense focus and high of pursuit. By recognizing it as normal, you take away some of its sting. Instead of panicking that something is wrong with you, you can say, "Ah, this is that post-achievement come-down I've heard about. It makes sense that I feel this way." That perspective alone begins the healing journey – because it replaces self-criticism with understanding.

Acknowledge the Feelings

Once you accept that the "success hangover" is normal, the next step is to acknowledge what you're feeling – openly and without judgment. This might sound simple, but for many high achievers it's surprisingly hard. You might be tempted to brush off or bury your emotions. Perhaps a voice in your head says, *"I shouldn't feel like this – I got exactly what I wanted!*

Snap out of it." Yet denying your feelings only pushes them into the shadows, where they can actually grow stronger or morph into anxiety. The healthiest move you can make right now is to face your emotions head-on. Give them a name, let them surface, and accept that they are there.

So, what *are* you feeling? Is it sadness, now that the excitement has faded? Is it anxiety about what comes next? Maybe it's a sense of emptiness or loss of purpose. You might even feel guilty or confused for having negative emotions at all when everyone expects you to be celebrating. Take a moment and really consider the swirl inside you. Identify each emotion and say it to yourself, or even out loud: "I feel empty," "I feel anxious," "I feel a bit lost." By naming the feeling, you shine a light on it. It's no longer this amorphous cloud making you uneasy; it becomes something you can understand and address.

A key part of acknowledging feelings is doing so without self-judgment. Remind yourself that *emotions are not moral.* Feeling down doesn't make you ungrateful or spoiled; it makes you human (as we've established). Imagine telling a friend about how you feel: a true friend wouldn't scold you, they'd probably put a hand on your shoulder and say, *"I get it. You've been through a lot – it's okay to feel what you feel."* You need to extend that same gentle understanding to yourself. Give yourself permission to feel whatever comes. It is okay to feel empty or low after achieving something significant. In a conversational tone, it's like telling yourself: *"Yes, you might feel low – and yes, that's actually okay."*

By openly acknowledging your feelings, you actually lessen their power over you. There's a popular saying in psychology: "What you resist, persists." It means that when we fight our emotions or try to suppress them, they often linger or intensify. Conversely, when you acknowledge an emotion, it tends to start loosening its grip. Think of emotions like ocean waves – if you stand rigid against a wave, it can knock you over, but if you relax and float, you ride it until it dissipates. In practical terms, this might mean allowing yourself a good cry if you need one, or admitting to a trusted confidant, "I know it sounds strange, but I actually feel a bit down after accomplishing that goal." You might be surprised how liberating and validating it is to simply speak your truth.

One technique that many people find helpful is journaling their feelings. When you have a jumble of emotions post-achievement, writing them down can be like opening a pressure valve. Try grabbing a notebook and free-writing about what finishing this journey felt like. Describe the high point and then describe the low point that followed. Write down any and all emotions – pride, sadness, relief, fear of the future, nostalgia for the process, whatever comes. Don't worry about being positive or logical; this journal is for your eyes only, a safe space to pour it out. Seeing your feelings in black and white can provide insight. You might notice, for example, that a lot of your sadness is actually about missing the *process* (the camaraderie of the team, the daily challenge, etc.), and not about the achievement itself. Realizations like that can help you understand what your heart is longing for now.

Above all, practice accepting your emotions as they are, without trying to "fix" them immediately. This acceptance is a powerful first step forward. It may feel counterintuitive – when something's wrong, don't we usually try to solve it right away? But emotional healing doesn't work that way. You can't "solve" feelings like a math problem. They need to be acknowledged and felt. Paradoxically, the fastest way *through* difficult feelings is to stop racing to escape them. When you simply say, *"Alright, I feel sad/ empty/ anxious right now and that feeling is allowed,"* you take away the shame or resistance that could be keeping that feeling stuck. You are facing the void rather than running from it, and that courage to face it will serve you immensely in the journey ahead.

Self-Compassion Over Self-Criticism

As a high achiever, you might be used to holding yourself to very high standards. That inner voice that drove you to succeed might also have a harsh edge – an Inner Critic that says "toughen up" or "don't be so weak." In this post-achievement slump, however, self-criticism will only dig the hole deeper. The antidote you need right now is self-compassion. This means treating yourself with the same kindness, empathy, and patience that you would offer to a dear friend or someone you care about.

Consider how you would react if someone you love came to you and said, "I achieved my dream, but now I just feel empty and depressed." Would you scold them and say, "How dare you feel that way? Toughen up!"? Of course not. You would likely listen, give them a hug, and reassure them that it's okay to feel that way and that they'll get through it. You might remind them of how hard they worked and suggest they deserve some rest. You'd probably encourage them gently, saying things like, "Be kind to yourself; you've been through a lot. It makes sense you're exhausted emotionally." Now, turn that same voice toward yourself. You deserve the same compassion you'd readily extend to others.

Self-compassion can be a game-changer, especially for people who are normally very hard on themselves. Research has shown that people who practice self-compassion tend to have lower anxiety and depression, and actually bounce back faster from setbacks. It's not self-indulgence or "babying" yourself – it's a healthy strategy for resilience. When that inner critic pipes up with, *"You don't have time for this, just get over it,"* you can respond with a kinder inner voice: *"Hey, I'm going through something right now. I need care, not criticism."* This conscious replacement of self-criticism with self-compassion might feel awkward at first, but it gets easier with practice, and the results are profound. You'll likely find your stress level goes down and your ability to cope goes up.

Here are a few practical ways to practice self-compassion during this period:

- **Speak to yourself kindly:** Pay attention to your self-talk. If you catch yourself saying harsh things internally ("I'm so pathetic for feeling this way"), stop and reframe. Imagine a close friend or mentor was listening – would they agree with that statement, or would they counter it with something kinder? Deliberately choose words you'd offer to a friend: "I'm human and it's okay to feel this. I did my best and I'm allowed to take a breather."

- **Give yourself permission to be imperfect:** High achievers often have trouble being anything less than 100%. But right now, you might not be operating at full capacity – and that's okay. If you're a little less productive or upbeat for a while, grant yourself that grace. Think of it like an athlete recovering from a marathon; you wouldn't expect them to sprint the day after a race. In the same way, you don't have to be at peak performance emotionally right after a major life event. Self-compassion means allowing yourself to recuperate without guilt.

- **Nurture yourself with small acts of care:** This might include physical care (like making sure you eat well, get enough sleep, maybe enjoying a long bath or a walk in nature) and emotional care (like watching a favorite comfort movie or calling a supportive friend). These are not frivolous activities; they are important signals to your brain that you are safe and cared for. When you treat yourself with kindness, you reinforce the feeling that you *matter* beyond just your accomplishments.

- **Journal or talk it out (without judgment):** We mentioned journaling as a way to acknowledge feelings; it's also a form of self-compassion because you're giving yourself a non-judgmental space to express. Alternatively, talk to someone you trust about how you feel, but choose someone who you know will be understanding. Sometimes voicing your struggles and hearing someone say "I get it, and I'm here for you" is incredibly soothing.

Remember that self-compassion is not the same as complacency. Some high achievers fear that if they go "too easy" on themselves, they'll lose their edge. In reality, being kind to yourself now will help you regain your strength sooner. Beating yourself up is not a motivating strategy; it usually just creates more pain and drains motivation. On the other hand, self-compassionate people tend to recover faster and feel more motivated *because* they haven't wasted energy on self-blame. Think of it this way: if you're injured, you heal faster with proper care, not by berating the injury. Similarly, for an emotional bruise like the post-success blues, care and kindness are the healing balm.

In embracing self-compassion, you reaffirm an important truth: your worth is not solely defined by your achievements. You are worthy of kindness and care simply because you are *you*. Achievements come and go, but you remain. Treating yourself kindly reinforces that your value isn't just in doing, but in being. This mindset will help rebuild your sense of self beyond this moment and set the stage for finding new purpose when you're ready.

Sit with the Discomfort

High achievers are doers by nature. When faced with a problem, the instinct is often to take action immediately. Feeling empty after a big win can seem like a problem begging for a solution: *"Quick, find the next goal! Stay busy so you don't feel this void!"* But as counterintuitive as it might be, the wisest move right now is to pause. Resist the urge to instantly fill the void with a new project or adrenaline rush. Instead, give yourself permission to *sit with the discomfort* for a while.

What does it mean to sit with discomfort? It means not rushing to escape the uneasy feelings, but rather allowing them to be present and observing them. This is a concept borrowed from mindfulness practices and therapy techniques – essentially, you're agreeing to spend a little time in this in-between space instead of sprinting out of it. Think of it like this: after climbing a very tall mountain, you don't rush to climb another the next day; you come down, rest at base camp, let your muscles recover, and reflect on the journey. That resting period is not wasted time – it's essential for your well-being and for integrating what you've experienced.

In the same way, after your big "mountain-top" achievement, a period of rest and reflection is not only okay, it's essential. You've expended a lot of effort – mental, emotional, perhaps physical – in reaching your goal. Your system needs to recuperate. If you immediately launch into the next chase, you risk burnout, or carrying unresolved feelings into your next endeavor. By sitting with the discomfort now, you ensure that when you do decide to climb the next mountain, you'll do it with a clear mind and a genuine motivation, rather than as an escape from sadness.

So practically, how can you spend this time? Start with the basics: truly rest. It's amazing how many driven individuals neglect rest. You might notice you're actually tired on a very literal level. Perhaps in the push to achieve, you skimped on sleep or constantly ran on adrenaline. Now is a time to *recharge your batteries*. Let yourself sleep in if you can, or go to bed earlier. Enjoy some unstructured downtime – the kind you might normally label "lazy," but is actually healing. Binge a few episodes of that show you missed, or spend a Sunday afternoon napping or lounging with a book. This downtime is not a guilty indulgence; frame it as part of your post-achievement recovery plan.

Next, reflect on the journey you've just been through. When the emotions aren't too raw, it can be very enlightening to gently analyze what this whole experience meant to you. While you're sitting with your feelings, ask yourself: *What did achieving this goal give me, and what did it not give me? What parts of the journey were the most fulfilling, and what parts were disappointing? What have I learned about myself through this process?* You might do this reflection in a journal, in a quiet walk in the park, or even discussing with a friend or mentor. The point isn't to immediately plan your next move, but to process the experience. Sometimes, during this reflection, you discover that the *process* of working toward the goal brought you a sense of purpose and camaraderie that you now miss. Or you might realize that some aspects of the goal weren't as satisfying as you expected, which is valuable information for your future. These insights are the gold nuggets hidden in the void – they help ensure that your next chapter will be informed by wisdom.

While you sit with discomfort, also pay attention to any small sparks of interest or joy that appear. With the big goal finished, you now have the mental space to notice little things again. Maybe in the past weeks you were too busy to enjoy cooking, and now making a meal slowly is oddly comforting. Or you find yourself drawn to an old hobby you had set aside. Perhaps you feel an urge to reconnect with friends or family you didn't have much time for. Allow yourself to explore these gentle urges without turning them into grand projects. This is a period of open exploration and quiet regeneration. It's somewhat like lying fallow – in agriculture, fields are sometimes left unplanted for a season to restore their fertility. In life, you too might need a "fallow" period after an intense harvest of achievement.

It's important to note that sitting with discomfort is not the same as doing nothing forever or wallowing without end. It has a purpose: to let the emotional dust settle and to listen to what your mind and body truly need next. Some days in this period might feel a bit aimless or awkward, especially if you're used to a packed agenda. That's okay – *tolerating a little aimlessness is part of the growth.* If you find yourself getting very antsy, you can set *gentle* structure: maybe you decide to exercise lightly a few times a week, or you schedule a short trip or a new class a month from now, not as a grand goal but as a way to explore and enjoy. The key is to avoid jumping into anything with the same intensity and stakes as the goal you just completed. Think "sabbatical" rather than "next mission" at this stage.

During this time, it may also help to seek perspective from others who have been through similar transitions. Talking to a fellow retiree, or another founder who sold their company, or a colleague who also finished a big project can remind you that this phase is typical and *temporary.* They might share how they coped and found new direction, which can be both comforting and illuminating. If you don't have people like that in your immediate circle, there are memoirs and biographies of successful individuals that candidly discuss the lull after success. Reading about their journeys can reassure you that *nearly everyone who strives greatly also struggles with "what now?"*. You'll see that those who ultimately thrive again are the ones who allowed themselves the grace of this in-between time rather than running from it.

Finally, consider incorporating some form of mindfulness or meditation into this period. Even a simple practice of sitting quietly for a few minutes each day, focusing on your breath or observing your thoughts, can help you stay present with your feelings without being overwhelmed by them. Mindfulness teaches us to notice thoughts and feelings as passing events, sort of like leaves floating down a stream, rather than identifying with each one. This can be very useful when you're sitting with uncomfortable emotions – you learn to watch them come and go without panicking that you'll feel this way forever. A meditation practice can be as simple as taking ten minutes in the morning to breathe deeply, or using a guided meditation app that helps with acceptance and letting go. It's a tool to center yourself when the void feels a bit too void-like.

Leaning into this downtime might feel strange at first, but trust that it's fertile ground. In this quiet, you are gradually recharging and clearing a space for the next phase of your life to emerge naturally. You're giving yourself the chance to discover what truly matters to you beyond the thrill of accolades. By not immediately filling the silence with noise, you might start to hear the whispers of new passions or the call to redefine your purpose in a way that's more fulfilling. When the time is right – whether in a few weeks or a couple of months – you will have the clarity and energy to decide on your next steps. And those next steps will be chosen out of genuine interest and meaning, not just a panicked attempt to avoid discomfort. Sitting with the discomfort now is an investment in a more purposeful future.

In facing the void after your summit, acceptance truly is the first step. By normalizing the post-achievement letdown, acknowledging your feelings, treating yourself with compassion, and giving yourself time to sit with the discomfort, you lay a strong foundation for whatever comes next. This chapter in your life – the one after "making it" – is just beginning. It might start quietly, even bleakly, but with acceptance, that quiet space becomes a canvas rather than a void. You are clearing the ground and tending to yourself, so that new purpose and identity can take root. Every great journey has a pause at the summit – a moment to catch your breath and take in the view, before descending into the next adventure. Consider this chapter that moment of pause. Embrace it, and trust that from acceptance will come the inspiration and direction for the path ahead. You have made it this far; now, by accepting where you are, you are making way for the next evolution of *you*.

Chapter 7

Rebuilding Purpose – Aligning with Values and Passions

After reaching a long-sought summit of success, many people are surprised to find themselves peering into a void rather than basking in endless satisfaction. You might recognize that hollow feeling: the project is finished, the trophy is won, the company is sold – and now *what*? Psychologists actually have a name for this letdown: post-achievement depression, often tied to the "arrival fallacy," which is the illusion that once you *arrive* at your big goal, you'll be permanently happy. In reality, the thrill is often fleeting. In one study, over 70% of people reported feeling *less happy* after achieving a significant goal than they had anticipated. It turns out the external accolades and finish-line moments don't automatically translate into lasting fulfillment. When the confetti settles, disappointment and aimlessness can creep in – *the Success Void*.

But take heart: this chapter is about filling that void by rebuilding your sense of purpose. Now that you've faced the initial emptiness and asked "What now?", it's time to rediscover what truly drives you on a deeper level. You'll learn to reconnect with your core "Why", expand your identity beyond any single accomplishment, and revive the passions and simple joys that make life rich. We'll also look at a real-life story of a high-powered achiever who found new purpose in down-to-earth ways.

By the end of this chapter, you should feel excited that a more meaningful, balanced chapter of life lies ahead – one grounded in your personal values rather than in external markers of success. Let's begin this rebuilding process step by step.

Reconnect with Your "Why"

When the initial celebration fades, it's crucial to reconnect with why you pursued that achievement in the first place. What was it about that goal that mattered to you on a personal level? What parts of the journey made you feel *alive*? By digging into these questions, you shift focus from the empty *end* of the road to the meaningful motivations that fueled you along the way. In other words, you start to anchor your purpose in internal values instead of external validation. This can be a powerful antidote to the arrival fallacy. After all, if chasing the trophy left you cold, maybe it's time to find warmth in the *reason* you were chasing it at all.

Take a moment to reflect on your own "why." Consider journaling or just thinking through prompts like: "What genuinely makes me happy day-to-day?" "Which moments or aspects of my big accomplishment felt most meaningful?" "Why was that goal important to me beyond the prestige or reward?" Often, you'll find that behind a professional milestone or award was a deeper personal value. For example, perhaps building your startup from scratch was gratifying not *because* of the money and title, but because it let you be creative, solve problems, or help others. Maybe winning a championship mattered so much to you because you love mastery and teamwork, not the medal itself. By identifying these core values – creativity, service, learning, community, excellence, whatever they may be – you get closer to your authentic purpose. Those values existed before the trophy, and they can guide you after it.

It's useful here to distinguish between intrinsic motivations and extrinsic rewards. Extrinsic rewards are things like praise, money, promotions – all the shiny outcomes that society applauds. Intrinsic motivations are the inner desires and values – like passion for the work, or the joy of engaging in a craft – that make the process itself fulfilling. Research in positive psychology suggests that when we align our goals with intrinsic values, we feel more satisfied and less disillusioned afterwards. In contrast, if we pursue something mostly for extrinsic reasons (say, social status) we're more prone to that "now what?" emptiness once we get it. As Tal Ben-Shahar (the psychologist who coined "arrival fallacy") points out, *expectations vs. reality* is a tricky thing – we imagine the external reward will change our life, but often it doesn't, at least not for long. The key is to find meaning in the process and principles you care about, not just the end result.

One strategy used in therapy (specifically Acceptance and Commitment Therapy, or ACT) is to help people clarify their core values and then align their actions to those values. Studies have found that *identifying what truly matters* to you and using it as a compass can enhance your overall well-being and satisfaction. Your "why" is essentially those things that truly matter. By reconnecting with it, you start to rebuild purpose not as a one-time goal to reach, but as a continuous guiding light.

Try this: Think back to why you set out on your successful journey in the beginning. Write down at least *three core values or motivations* that drove you. Did you want to make a positive impact on your community? Did you crave artistic expression? Were you seeking freedom or security for your family? There are no wrong answers – just be honest with yourself about what lights you up inside.

Grounding yourself in your "why" does a few important things. First, it shifts your focus from *outcome* to meaning. The achievement isn't an end in itself now – it's part of a bigger picture of living according to your values. This mindset can immediately soften the sense of aimlessness. For example, instead of, "I climbed the mountain and now I'm depressed it's over," you might realize, "I climbed it because I love adventure and personal growth – so what's my next adventure that fulfills that love?" You start seeing new paths forward that honor the same values. Second, focusing on why the accomplishment mattered helps you appreciate the journey you had, not just the finish line. Perhaps the daily discipline of training or the camaraderie with colleagues was the real gold. Savor those aspects – they're clues to what you find purposeful. Third, reconnecting with your why reminds you that *you are more than any one victory.* You stand for something – whether it's innovation, compassion, learning, or anything else – and that *transcends a single milestone.* Your purpose can thus be an ongoing story, not a one-time event.

On a practical level, once you've identified or rediscovered your core motivations, you can start to set new goals that align with them. Importantly, these new goals don't have to be as grand or externally impressive as your last achievement – they just need to resonate with your values. If your last goal was largely for external approval, consider making the next one more personally meaningful. For instance, if you won an award in your industry that left you oddly empty, maybe your next goal is to mentor young people in the field – something aligned with a value of generosity and legacy. If you sold your company and felt lost, perhaps your "why" was actually building things and working with a close-knit team, so you could find that by investing in a new venture or even helping others start businesses. By reconnecting with why it all mattered, you create a roadmap for *what's next* that is fulfilling in itself. As one executive coach put it, *"Set new objectives that are meaningful and aligned with your values"* – that way, the journey towards them will feel worthwhile, not just the moment you arrive.

In summary, meaning > accolades. Take time to soul-search and identify the values, passions, and motivations that give you energy. That internal "why" is going to be the foundation on which you build the next phase of life. It shifts your mindset from *"I need another mountain to climb to feel happy"* (which is the hamster wheel of achievement for achievement's sake) to *"I need the right mountain – one that aligns with my purpose."* With your why in hand, you're no longer adrift; you have an inner compass again. And that is a huge first step in rebuilding purpose.

Expand Your Identity

Another crucial step in finding purpose beyond your big win is learning to expand your identity. High achievers often fall into the trap of defining themselves almost entirely by that one role or accomplishment. It's no wonder that when the project ends or you step off the podium, you feel like you've lost *yourself*. In truth, you are not just your job title, gold medal, or achievement – and remembering this can be profoundly liberating. It's time to diversify how you see yourself and reclaim the *many* facets of your identity that make you whole.

Think of it this way: your achievement was just one chapter in the book of you. Now you have the opportunity to write new chapters and develop other characters in your story. Are you a leader at work? Sure – but perhaps you're also a parent, a friend, a mentor, a traveler, a creative soul, a lifelong learner. Those roles and qualities are just as real and important as any business card or trophy. In fact, embracing multiple identities can protect you from the devastating emptiness that comes if one identity disappears. Productivity guru Tim Ferriss calls it "identity diversification" – investing your self-worth in a variety of areas (relationships, hobbies, personal growth, etc.) so that *if one area goes south, you're not completely emotionally wrecked*. It's like diversifying a financial portfolio: don't put all your eggs (or self-esteem) in one basket.

Consider a powerful example. In a Tony Robbins seminar recounted by writer Mark Manson, a formerly successful finance executive shared that after he lost a fortune, he felt he had nothing left to live for. Why? Because, as he admitted, he had invested all of his identity in being "the money guy." He literally believed his *only* value as a person was his ability to make money for himself and others. He didn't see himself as a loving father, or a witty friend, or a person with any other talents – so when the money was gone, *his entire sense of self vanished*. It's a heart-wrenching story, but it perfectly illustrates the danger of a one-dimensional identity. If you hang your self-worth entirely on a single hook, you're left in free fall when that hook gives way.

Now contrast that with someone who has a more balanced self-concept. For instance, take an Olympic athlete who eventually retires from competition. The ones who struggle the most are those who think "I *am* only an athlete." But many former athletes find peace by expanding their identity – they realize they can be mentors, businesspeople, artists, parents, students, or advocates. Tennis legend Serena Williams, for example, spoke about "evolving" away from tennis to focus on being a mother and an entrepreneur. She recognized that while she will always be proud of being a tennis champion, she is also much more: a parent, a business founder, a philanthropist. By embracing those roles, Serena essentially widened the foundation of her identity so it's not solely propped up by her sports accolades. This kind of shift is available to all of us, famous or not.

Even top corporate leaders have learned this lesson. Indra Nooyi, the former CEO of PepsiCo, once shared a memorable piece of advice her mother gave her: *"You may be the president of PepsiCo, but when you come home, you are a wife and a mother and a daughter. Nobody can take your place. So leave that crown in the garage."*. In other words, *don't bring your CEO ego into the house.* Remember that you have roles in life where your title and achievements don't matter – you are irreplaceable for being *you* to your family and friends. Nooyi admitted that despite an amazing career, there were moments she wished she'd spent more time with her children and family. She has emphasized that work is just one part of who you are;

your loved ones, your values, and how you impact others define you far more profoundly. This perspective can be a salve for the success void: it reminds you that *your inherent worth isn't in what you've achieved, but in who you are to the people and world around you.*

So how do you expand your identity in practice? Start by acknowledging all the roles you already have. Make a list of the things you are besides "the award-winner" or "the boss." You might list roles (like friend, sibling, volunteer) and traits or passions (nature lover, history buff, musician, mentor, traveler, etc.). Seeing this list written out can be eye-opening – it's evidence that you are a multi-dimensional human. Next, give yourself permission to prioritize some of those other identities. Perhaps during your push for the big achievement, you sidelined a lot of these roles (e.g. hardly spending time with family, or neglecting your creative side). Now is the time to rebalance. Consciously devote time and energy to aspects of yourself that were on hold. Maybe schedule regular meetups with friends, or commit to an evening a week in which you are *"not a CEO"* but just a parent at the playground or a novice painter in a class.

By diversifying your identity, you also cushion yourself against future ups and downs. If one aspect of your life takes a hit, you have others to draw strength from. Psychologists note that when one's identity is overly tied to a single pursuit, its completion can spur a crisis of uncertainty. But if your identity is spread across family, hobbies, community, and work, a change in one domain (say, retiring from your career) won't leave you feeling like a nobody – you'll still have many somebodies to be. As personal development author Mark Manson writes, *"It's smart to diversify your identity – invest your self-esteem in a variety of areas… so that when one goes south, you're not completely screwed over and emotionally wrecked."* It may sound a bit blunt, but it's true!

One beautiful way to expand identity is to refocus on the impact you want to have rather than the job you do. Recall the author of the 5.12 Solutions leadership blog we mentioned earlier: after completing his grueling bike race and feeling that post-accomplishment void, he reflected that he wanted to redefine his identity "not attached so much to the *'what I do'* but to the impact I want to make in this world". This is a profound shift. It means seeing yourself not just as "I am a lawyer" or "I am an Olympian," but rather "I am someone who [mentors youth / fights for justice / spreads joy / creates beauty / etc.]." When you broaden the definition in that way, it becomes easier to find new avenues to live out that identity. For example, if you identify as someone who wants to make a positive impact, you could do that in any number of roles – through charity work, coaching others, launching a foundation, writing a book, or simply being a kind leader in whatever you do next. Your identity becomes about your values and the effect you have, not the specific vehicle you used to have. This mindset keeps you future-oriented and adaptable. You might even say it helps you build a legacy identity – one that isn't chained to a single accomplishment, but is instead anchored in the kind of person you choose to be.

It may also help to seek out stories of others who reinvented or expanded themselves after reaching the top. There are plenty of inspiring examples across different fields. Some retired military generals have found purpose in humanitarian work or teaching. Former government leaders often take on new identities as authors, diplomats, or champions of causes (think of Nobel Peace laureate Malala Yousafzai – not a "former student" defined by one struggle, but an ongoing activist for girls' education). In business, we have figures like Jack Ma, the founder of Alibaba, who stepped down from his $400-billion company and declared he would dedicate his post-retirement days to philanthropy and education in rural China. Ma, who was once an English teacher, shifted his identity towards being an *educator and philanthropist*, channeling his influence to support rural teachers and agriculture. At the same time, Jack Ma also allowed his playful personal interests to flourish – while he was still leading Alibaba, he famously would sing pop songs at company events and even took up painting; he called himself a "young artist at heart," showing that even billionaires can have alter-egos in music and art. These facets were always part of him, and after retiring as chairman, he had more space to live them out (one of his paintings sold for millions at auction – clearly a serious hobby!). The point is: *you too contain multitudes.*

Expanding your identity beyond your past achievement brings a wonderful side effect: resilience. Life after a summit has its highs and lows, but if your sense of self is grounded in many things, you'll weather the changes better. You'll also likely find more happiness. People who engage in multiple roles and communities (family, social, creative, etc.) tend to report greater life satisfaction, because successes and support in one area can buffer challenges in another. So give yourself permission to be more than "the successful one." Be a *whole person*. Embrace being a rookie at something new, or being "just another volunteer" in a group, or being a supportive family member. Those experiences will enrich you and remind you that *your identity is a mosaic*, not a statue carved from a single stone.

Revive Passions and Hobbies

Reigniting your passion for activities outside of your main career or achievement is one of the most practical – and enjoyable – ways to rediscover purpose. Think of this as diversifying not just your identity on paper, but how you actually spend your time and derive joy. When you were laser-focused on that big goal, there's a good chance you put some hobbies or simple pleasures on the back burner. Now is the time to bring them back into your life, or try new ones that spark your curiosity. By doing so, you expand the sources of meaning in your daily routine, so that your life's purpose isn't solely defined by *that one accomplishment* or work alone.

Psychologists often advise people to *"increase your sources of reinforcement"* – in plain terms, to have multiple things in life that give you positive feelings, pride, or enjoyment. If all your dopamine was coming from work, for example, it's important to cultivate other activities that can also light you up. Engaging in hobbies has been shown to reduce stress, improve mood, and even help with depression. In fact, hobbies help you form a life outside of work or achievement. They let you relax and do something you enjoy *without any pressure from the outside world*. There's no performance review for baking sourdough bread, no world ranking for hiking in the woods, no gold medal for tinkering on the guitar in your living room – and that's *precisely* why these activities can be so fulfilling. They are for you, not for applause. Paradoxically, doing things "just for fun" can remind you that life is meant to be enjoyed, not just conquered.

Revisit the past interests you sidelined. Did you once love painting, cooking, writing poetry, playing basketball at the park, or traveling just for exploration? Give yourself permission to do those things again, even if it feels indulgent. Or maybe there's something you've *always wanted* to try but never had time for – gardening, learning a new language, taking a dance class, you name it. This is a perfect moment to start. You might be amazed at how a dormant passion can flare back to life and energize you. For example, a former high-powered executive might find immense joy in getting her hands dirty in a community garden, growing vegetables and flowers with a local group. It's a humble activity compared to running a company, but working with nature and neighbors could deliver a sense of peace and tangible satisfaction that quarterly earnings never did. Or an ex-professional athlete could take up photography as a beginner, discovering a whole new creative world where he's not "the star" but just happily learning and improving. These endeavors provide *fresh sources of achievement* – smaller scale, maybe, but still meaningful. You finish a woodworking project and feel proud. You volunteer at an animal shelter and feel needed. These feelings cumulatively rebuild a sense of purpose.

There's science to back this up. Leisure activities and hobbies have been linked to greater happiness and even improved work performance in the long run. Engaging in something purely because you *want* to (not because you *have* to) produces positive emotions and a sense of autonomy. Hobbies provide us with a sense of purpose, accomplishment, and joy on a very personal level. They tap into intrinsic motivation – you do it because it matters to you or it's fun, which is incredibly nourishing for the psyche. Moreover, hobbies often put us into a state of "flow," that focused blissful state where you lose track of time because you're so engaged. Whether it's cycling, playing piano, or baking, that flow state is like a mini-vacation for the mind, a reset that can make the rest of life feel more balanced.

Importantly, cultivating interests outside your main achievement protects you from putting all your eggs in one basket of meaning. As we discussed with identity, if your only source of pride or enjoyment was your career or that big win, then of course you feel empty when it's over. But if you have a rich tapestry of activities and relationships, no single thread going slack will leave you purposeless. A study on work-life balance found that people with serious hobbies unrelated to their job often coped better with stress and transitions. It's as if a hobby creates a parallel track of purpose. For instance, a doctor who also sings in a choir or plays in a band has another identity and community to draw joy from, which can be a refuge when work is tough or when retirement comes. Psychologist *Sal Silvester* (from the 5.12 Solutions blog) lists "Diversify Your Interests" as a key strategy to overcome post-success doldrums – *"Explore hobbies or activities unrelated to your achievement, so that your identity expands beyond what you do to the impact you want to make."* In practice, that might mean if you were a tech CEO, join a weekend hiking club and just be a nature enthusiast on Saturdays; if you were a decorated soldier now home, pick up painting or join a cooking class where you're a student again. These shifts broaden how you experience yourself and life.

Let's not forget the simple joy factor. Doing things "just because" can reignite your childlike enthusiasm. Remember when you were a kid and you did stuff with no thought of productivity – climbing trees, sketching cartoons, building model planes – hours would fly by and you felt alive. We all have an inner child still, and often that child hasn't had recess in a while because we've been "too busy." So give yourself some playtime. It's not frivolous; it's actually essential for a well-rounded sense of self. Many therapists will tell you that play and creativity are restorative. They remind us life is more than checklists and milestones.

Also, hobbies can lead to social connections and community, which is another pillar of purpose. Join a club, a class, or an online group related to your interest and you may meet people you wouldn't have otherwise. Those new relationships can be very enriching. Imagine you take up woodworking and start attending a local woodworkers' guild – you could end up with a whole new circle of friends who see you not as "former Vice President So-and-So" but as that friendly person who's also learning to carve bowls. Engaging with people on the basis of shared passion (instead of shared ambition) can be refreshingly authentic. It also reinforces that you have value to give and lessons to learn in multiple arenas of life.

If you're not sure where to start with reviving or finding a passion, think about what *sparks your curiosity or makes you lose track of time*. Think of times you've felt a playful excitement or deep calm while doing something. That's your clue. It could be anything: cooking, hiking, writing, painting, gardening, playing an instrument, traveling, martial arts, restoring old cars, salsa dancing, photography, volunteering with kids or the elderly, learning about astronomy — the list is endless. The key is *the process should feel rewarding*, not just the end result. You don't ever have to be the world's best gardener or painter; the point is to enjoy it and find meaning in the doing. One retired CEO said that volunteering at a community garden every week "gave me back more than I could possibly give" — she found that nurturing plants and chatting with neighbors while pulling weeds made her feel grounded and useful in a totally new way. Another former elite athlete took up hiking and described how summiting small peaks with friends for fun actually brought a purer happiness than some of his competitive victories, because there was no pressure — just a love of nature and camaraderie.

Psychologically, what we're doing by reviving passions and hobbies is expanding the definition of a "successful day." It's not only a successful day if you made a business deal or received an accolade. It can also be a successful day if you baked a beautiful loaf of bread, or finished reading a novel, or had a great jam session on the piano, or helped at the local food pantry. Those things count. They count to *you* and that's enough. Over time, these little joys and accomplishments weave a safety net of purpose under your life. They ensure that even if one big thing is over, you wake up knowing there are many sources of happiness and meaning you can tap into.

In sum, don't underestimate the power of passions and hobbies. They're not "extra" – they're an integral part of a purposeful life. A life well-lived has room for work, love, and play. By reviving old pleasures and discovering new ones, you remind yourself that there is *more to life to love*. This greatly diminishes the success void because your emotional "eggs" are now in many baskets. Each day can hold a spark of purpose, whether it's the day you mentor someone at work (purpose through impact), the evening you experiment with a new recipe (purpose through creativity), or the weekend you go camping with family (purpose through connection and adventure). Bit by bit, as you nurture these diverse passions, you will feel your inner fire rekindling. That hollow space left after the summit will begin to fill with curiosity, delight, and renewed motivation for the journey ahead.

Story: The Executive Who Found Balance

Let's bring these ideas to life with a real-world narrative. Meet Rajita, a fictional composite drawn from true stories of high-flyers who hit the success void. Rajita was a hard-charging executive – the CEO of a global retail company – who spent 25 years climbing the corporate ladder. In her early 50s, she achieved the pinnacle of her career: she led a major company turnaround, was lauded in the business press, and ultimately negotiated a lucrative merger that effectively "completed" her mission. At the celebration party, colleagues toasted to her accomplishments and her family beamed with pride. By all external measures, Rajita had *made it*. She decided to step down at the top of her game, imagining a blissful early retirement after such a summit.

But within a few weeks of handing over the reins, Rajita woke up feeling completely adrift. Without the daily flood of emails, meetings, and decisions, her days stretched emptily. She didn't have to rush to the office – and paradoxically, that made her feel anxious and unimportant. The phone stopped ringing; her calendar was blank. She described it to a friend as "like standing in a quiet field after years in a noisy stadium – peaceful but also eerily *alone*." The victory she'd worked so hard for left her with a startling question: Who am I now? She realized that for decades she had thought of herself almost entirely as "Rajita, the CEO." Now that title was gone. Sure, she had more than enough money and a wall full of awards, but those didn't tell her how to get out of bed in the morning with a sense of purpose. Rajita had entered her own success void.

At first, Rajita tried to fill the void by doing what she was used to: achieving. She signed up for a couple of industry boards and threw herself into advising a startup. Those were worthwhile endeavors, but if she was honest, she was doing them mostly to feel relevant and busy. It was like she was clinging to shreds of her old identity. After a few months, she felt burned out *again* and oddly still unfulfilled. In a moment of frustration, Rajita admitted to her husband that she was feeling depressed. "I should be happy, but I'm not. I don't know what to do with myself," she said. This candid confession was a turning point. It pushed her to remember why she had worked so hard all those years. What had she neglected or postponed during her career? What had she always said she'd do "someday"? Two things immediately came to mind: *family* and *community*.

94

Rajita realized that while she had provided a great life for her family, she hadn't been as present as she wanted. And she had always told herself that one day she would "give back to the community" more directly. These were her core values peeking through: she deeply cared about her loved ones and about making a positive impact on ordinary people's lives. In the past, those values were channeled into being a responsible provider and a charitable donor. But now she had the time and freedom to live those values more fully. This epiphany was Rajita reconnecting with her "why." She remembered that beneath her career ambition, she genuinely believed in uplifting others and creating a sense of belonging – that's what made her feel alive, even at work.

So Rajita made a bold decision: instead of jumping into another high-powered role to chase away the emptiness, she would deliberately slow down and realign her life with her values. Practically, that meant focusing on being more present with her family and finding a form of service that was close to her heart. The first changes were simple but profound. She started having long breakfast conversations with her college-aged daughters, something she never had time for before. She began joining her husband on evening walks around the neighborhood. Initially, she felt a bit "unproductive" doing these things, but to her surprise, they filled her days with warmth. She was reconnecting with her identity as a mother, wife, sister, and friend – roles that had always been there but were now front and center. Her daughters later told her how much it meant that she was *"truly there, not checking emails, not rushing off"* during those breakfasts. Rajita realized she was making an impact in the most important circle of all: her family. That alone gave her a sense of purpose that no award could match.

Parallel to this, Rajita looked for ways to engage with her local community. She remembered a community center in town that ran a community garden and food program for neighborhood residents. Gardening had been a beloved hobby of hers in childhood, taught by her father, though she'd abandoned it in the busy years. With a mix of nerves and excitement, Rajita showed up one Saturday morning at the community garden as a volunteer. The coordinator handed her a pair of gloves and set her to work alongside other volunteers of all ages – teenagers earning service hours, retired folks, even some of her former company's junior employees who didn't realize who she was outside of her power suit. In the dirt and sunshine, everyone was simply equal, just neighbors working together. Rajita spent the morning pulling weeds and tending tomato plants. It was the most physically tired and mentally relaxed she had felt in ages.

As weeks went by, this volunteering became Rajita's new passion. Every Saturday, she'd be out there in jeans and a floppy hat, chatting with the regulars. She befriended a widowed elderly woman who taught her how to prune roses, and in turn she found herself informally mentoring a shy teen who came to help out (eventually guiding the girl on applying to college, which was immensely rewarding for them both). The community garden produce went to a food pantry, and Rajita sometimes helped distribute baskets of vegetables to families in need. Handing a bag of fresh produce to a struggling mother and seeing genuine gratitude in her eyes – that gave Rajita a fulfillment as deep as any business deal she'd ever done. It struck her: this was *impact*, immediate and human. She was aligning with the values of community and kindness that had always mattered to her.

Over time, Rajita's identity expanded in the eyes of others and, most importantly, in her own eyes. She wasn't "retired CEO (restless)" anymore. She was "community volunteer," "gardener," "mentor," "mom." She even revived her love of music by joining a local choir, just for fun. On Tuesday nights, she became a humble alto in a group of 30 singers, none of whom cared that she used to run a big company – they cared that she showed up to rehearse harmonies. It was humbling and exhilarating to start as a novice in something new. Rajita joked that learning to hit the high notes in Latin lyrics was a lot harder than learning corporate finance, but it made her feel young and challenged in the best way.

The more Rajita diversified her life, the more the lingering sadness about her past achievement faded. She reflected that selling her company had been meaningful – it secured her employees' futures and satisfied investors – but it wasn't the *only* meaningful thing in her life. In fact, she began to see that her career success had given her a platform and resources that she could now use in service of what she truly cared about. For example, she initiated a program at the community center to provide small scholarships to the teen volunteers, using some of her own money and her business connections to fund it. This project lit her up; it combined her executive skills with her community passion. In essence, she *redefined success* for herself. It was no longer about leading a Fortune 500 company; it was about living according to her principles of family, community, and growth. Each day she asked, "What good can I do today?" and found an answer – whether it was helping her daughter move into a new apartment, giving career advice to a young neighbor, or simply perfecting her homemade chai recipe to share with friends (yes, she took up a bit of cooking too!).

Rajita's story shows a real-life blueprint of rebuilding purpose beyond the boardroom or spotlight. By reconnecting with her "why" (valuing family and community), expanding her identity (from CEO to volunteer, mentor, hobbyist, parent), and reviving passions and new hobbies (gardening, music, service), she filled the void that had once scared her. Importantly, she didn't do this overnight. There were moments she doubted herself or felt nostalgic for her old life. But whenever that happened, she remembered her values and leaned into the *present* activities that mattered to her. Over a couple of years, she crafted a life that was arguably more balanced and happy than when she was at her career peak. She still used her talents – but in ways aligned with her heart.

If you saw Rajita now, you might not immediately guess her past prestige, and she's perfectly okay with that. She'll gladly tell you about the heirloom tomatoes she's growing or gush about how her choir performed at the local library opening. Her eyes light up with the same kind of passion she once had in the boardroom – except this time, the passion is spread across *many simple joys* rather than one big goal. And here's the kicker: by rebuilding her purpose in this holistic way, Rajita actually feels *freer and more secure* in herself. She knows who she is, success or failure, job or no job. She's guided by her values and energized by her interests. The "success void" is no match for a life so richly textured with meaning.

The Takeaway: Whether you are a retired CEO like Rajita, an athlete at the end of your career, or anyone who has climbed a personal Everest, you can find purpose again by aligning with what truly matters to you. Reconnect with your why, expand your identity beyond that one peak, and dive into passions that make you happy to be alive. Purpose is not a fixed destination; it's a living, evolving thing, built through everyday actions and commitments. In the aftermath of "making it," you get to rediscover that *you* are so much more than that one mountain. Your summit was just one view – now you have the whole horizon to explore. By grounding yourself in values, nurturing multiple aspects of your identity, and embracing passions for their own sake, you will slowly but surely fill that success void with a new sense of meaning. And this time, it won't be tied to a single achievement, but to the very essence of who you are and the life you're creating. That is purpose reborn – a purpose no triumph or loss can ever take away from you.

Chapter 8

New Mountains to Climb – Setting Meaningful Goals Anew

A **Peak Behind, a Horizon Ahead:** Standing atop a great achievement can be a moment of exhilaration – you've reached your personal "summit," basked in the thin, heady air of success. But once the initial thrill fades, many high-achievers find themselves gazing out at a wide-open horizon and wondering, *"Now what?"* The climb that consumed your days is over, and the quiet that follows can feel unsettling. This chapter is about charting your way forward from that peak. Consider it an invitation to envision new mountains to climb – but this time, with greater mindfulness and purpose. Instead of chasing the next big thing just to chase it, you'll learn how to set fresh goals that genuinely excite you and reflect the person you are *now*, not the person you used to be. The aim is to transform that post-summit void into an open road full of possibilities. With a new vision grounded in your values, a playful approach to exploring interests, and a focus on the journey rather than the destination, you can find purpose again even after you've "made it." Life is far from over after a big win; in many ways, a richer, more meaningful adventure is just beginning.

A New Vision: Goals That Reflect Who You Are Now

After a major accomplishment, it's natural to feel both pride and an odd sense of loss. The goal that guided you for so long has been met, and you might feel as though you've left an old self behind on that mountaintop. In fact, you *have* changed – the person who achieved that success isn't the exact same person who started the journey years ago. Your experiences have reshaped you, your priorities may have evolved, and perhaps your view of success itself has grown more nuanced. This is why setting **a new vision** for your future is so important: it ensures your next chapter aligns with the person you've become.

Take a moment to imagine the climber who's conquered Everest. After the descent, they can't remain at that peak forever – they must come down and ask what's next. Some climbers fall into a slump, chasing ever-higher summits in vain or feeling aimless once the highest peak is behind them. Others, however, pause and realize there are many other mountains and adventures that can be just as rewarding in different ways. They might choose a new kind of expedition that speaks to passions they've discovered along the way, or even chart a completely different course in life. The key is that their new goal grows out of genuine interest and meaning, not out of a desperate need to replicate the old high or impress onlookers.

In redefining your vision, give yourself permission to set goals that truly excite you from the inside. This might sound obvious, but high achievers often fall into the trap of picking goals based on who they *used* to be or what others expect of them. For example, an executive who just led a company to a successful merger might think their next step *has* to be an even bigger corporate role – because that's what their past self-wanted or what peers assume. But maybe over the years, that executive has developed a new passion for social entrepreneurship, or a longing to spend more time with family, or a curiosity about a different field entirely. A new vision could involve pivoting to start a charitable foundation, writing a memoir, or launching a boutique startup in a creative industry – if that is what genuinely lights a spark now. What matters is that the goal reflects who you are today and what you honestly find meaningful, not what would simply look good on paper.

This shift may require overcoming the reflex to seek external approval. After achieving something big, you might feel pressure to outdo yourself or to choose a next goal that maintains a certain image of success. But chasing goals for the sake of status or applause is a recipe for emptiness. Many Olympic gold medalists, for instance, have spoken about the depression that hit them after their wins. They had been aiming to please coaches, country, or crowd – and once the medals were hung and the cheers faded, they realized those external accolades couldn't sustain them for long. Swimmer Michael Phelps, the most decorated Olympian in history, admitted that after his triumphs he felt lost and struggled with depression. His turning point came when he started focusing on personal well-being and advocacy that mattered to him (such as mental health awareness), rather than accumulating more medals for the world's approval. The lesson for all of us is powerful: goals chosen to impress others will rarely nourish your soul once the spotlight moves on. Goals chosen to fulfill you, on the other hand, can keep you energized through both success and setback.

So, as you envision your next "mountain," be bold in choosing something that matters to *you*. Maybe it's a career change into a field you've always been curious about, even if it's completely different from your previous path. Maybe it's a creative project – painting, music, writing, design – that you never had time for while you were busy building your legacy. It could be a personal challenge, like learning a new language or training for your first marathon at 50, purely for the joy of growth. It could even be less about *achievement* and more about *experience*, such as traveling to immerse yourself in different cultures or dedicating time to raise your children or grandchildren now that you have the freedom. The form of the goal isn't what makes it worthwhile; it's the feeling it stirs in you. Does it excite you? Does it feel meaningful in your gut? Those are the signals that you're onto something real. Whether your next chapter is flashy or quiet, conventional or unexpected, doesn't matter. Quality of purpose far outweighs quantity of accolades. It's far better to pursue a single goal that fills you with a sense of purpose than a dozen aims that leave you cold.

Consider the story of a renowned tech entrepreneur who sold her startup for a fortune. On paper, she'd "made it" beyond her wildest dreams. But in the months after the sale, she fell into a funk – the daily drive that woke her up each morning was gone, and she felt useless despite her wealth. Friends and onlookers suggested she simply start another big company to top the last. Instead, she took a step back and did some soul-searching. She realized that the aspect of her work she loved most was mentoring young creators and that one of her core values was community. With this new self-awareness, she set a very different kind of goal: she launched an incubator for socially conscious startups, investing in and guiding a new generation of entrepreneurs. It wasn't as high-profile as her previous venture, and it certainly wasn't about making more money — it was about doing something that aligned with her *current* values and passions. The result? She found herself waking up energized again, excited for each day's challenges. Her new vision gave her life a fresh meaning because it was authentic to who she had become.

Your new vision might not involve such a dramatic pivot, but it should capture whatever feels authentically exciting and significant to you now. Maybe you're still passionate about your primary field but want to approach it in a more meaningful way — say, shifting from a for-profit focus to a role where you can mentor others or innovate for social good. Or maybe you realize your heart is pulling you toward a long-neglected dream outside of work, like dedicating time to an art form or a humanitarian cause. Trust that instinct. You have earned the freedom to choose a path not out of necessity, but out of desire and conviction. Craft a vision for the future that, when you think about it, makes you feel a warm sense of *yes, this is right.*

As you do this, remember that you don't need to have the entire journey mapped out. A vision is a direction, not a detailed itinerary. Sir Edmund Hillary, after conquering Everest, devoted much of his later life to helping build schools and hospitals for the Sherpa communities in

Nepal. He didn't need another literal mountain to prove himself; he chose goals that expressed his values of gratitude and service. His new "mountains" were humanitarian projects that may not have been as glamorous as scaling a peak, but were deeply meaningful to him and to countless others. Hillary's story teaches us that a fulfilling next goal often grows naturally from our evolving sense of purpose. Envision a future that excites you and honors who you are – that is your new north star.

Align Goals with Values: Connecting Your Aims to What Matters Most

How can you be confident that a new goal will truly fulfill you and not lead to another hollow victory? The answer lies in aligning your goals with your core values. Values are the principles and beliefs that you hold most dear – the elements of life you find inherently worthwhile. In Chapter 7, you took time to identify those core values. Now it's time to put them front and center as you consider what to pursue next. By ensuring your next endeavor is *value-driven*, you greatly increase the chance that the journey will feel rich and rewarding, not empty.

Think of values as your personal compass. When you were striving for past achievements, you might have occasionally lost sight of that compass – it's easy to do when we get caught up in external definitions of success. Now, after experiencing the highs and lows of reaching a big milestone, you have the opportunity to recalibrate. Ask yourself: What truly matters to me at this stage of my life? What principles or passions do I want to express in my day-to-day activities? The goals you choose should serve as vehicles for living out those answers.

Let's say, for example, that through reflection you've realized *family* is one of your top values. Perhaps during your climb to success, family time was sacrificed for long hours at the office or on the road. If family is deeply important to you now, then any new goal should honor that. This could mean setting boundaries around work to be present at home, or even choosing a goal that *involves* family. Maybe you set an objective to take each of your children on a special trip, or you start a small family business with your spouse, or you commit to a project to trace your family genealogy. These are goals that might not sound like traditional "achievements" to outsiders, but they are tremendously meaningful because they let you live your value of family in a concrete way. The fulfillment you get from them will far surpass any fleeting applause from a goal that kept you away from loved ones.

Consider another person, a high-powered executive who identifies *health* and *well-being* as core values that had been neglected. Perhaps after years of corporate success, he finds himself out of shape or stressed out, and he yearns to reconnect with a healthier lifestyle. For him, a meaningful next goal could be something like training for a triathlon at age 60, or simply adopting a routine of hiking and meditation every weekend. To the outside world, that might not look as "big" as running a company, but for him it aligns perfectly with what he values now. Each training session or peaceful morning walk becomes rewarding in itself. He's not chasing a trophy for others to admire; he's pursuing well-being because it genuinely matters to him. In doing so, he finds a sense of accomplishment far deeper than any accolades from his business life.

Perhaps *creativity* or *learning* is your core value. If so, consider goals that immerse you in those pursuits. If creativity drives you, your next project might be finally starting that novel or building furniture in your workshop or taking an improv class. If lifelong learning is a value, maybe you enroll in courses in a subject that fascinates you – not to earn another degree for prestige, but simply to expand your mind and satisfy your curiosity. One retired lawyer we know found immense joy in signing up for a beginner's coding bootcamp; another took a deep dive into classical music by learning to play the piano. These goals were worthwhile because they resonated with their inner values of growth and creativity. Each small milestone – a functioning piece of code, a song practiced until it flowed – gave as much satisfaction as any courtroom victory, because it was aligned with who they truly are.

Psychological research supports the power of value-aligned goals. Studies have found that when people pursue goals that fit their authentic interests and values (sometimes called "self-concordant goals" by researchers), they experience greater motivation and satisfaction throughout the process. In other words, if your heart is in it from the start, you're more likely to enjoy the journey and feel proud of the outcome. On the flip side, goals that conflict with your values or are chosen for external rewards tend to leave you feeling empty, even if you achieve them. Many people have learned this the hard way: the corporate manager who aimed for a promotion mainly because of the prestige discovers that the new title didn't make them happier – in fact, it pulled them further from the kind of work-life balance they value. By contrast, the manager who maybe took a lateral step or a pay cut to work on a project that aligns with their environmental values might end each day feeling more at peace and energized. The alignment makes the difference.

When picking your next goal, it can be helpful to do a quick "values check." Write down your potential goal and then list which core values it connects to. If you struggle to find any, that's a red flag – maybe the goal needs to be adjusted or replaced. If you can clearly say, for example, "This goal of starting a community garden speaks to my values of sustainability, community, and creativity," then you've got a strong foundation. The more value boxes a goal checks, the more intrinsically meaningful it will feel. And when challenges arise – as they always do – those core values will act like a well of strength to draw from. You're much less likely to abandon a goal that resonates with your deepest convictions, because it's not just about achieving something out there; it's about honoring something in *here* (your heart, your identity).

Another benefit of value-aligned goals is that they redefine success in a healthier way. Instead of measuring success purely by external metrics (money made, awards won, applause given), you start measuring it by how well you are living out what matters to you. For instance, say one of your values is *generosity*. If you embark on a goal to mentor three young professionals in your field, there's no public fanfare in that. You won't get a plaque or a magazine profile for "Mentor of the Year." But every session you spend guiding those mentees will reaffirm your generous spirit and likely bring you immense personal satisfaction. Success, in this context, becomes the quiet sense that you're making a difference and living true to yourself. That is a success that external events can't take away from you, because it's rooted in your values and actions.

To align goals with values, it may help to recall specific moments from your past achievement journey that felt truly fulfilling. What made those moments satisfying? Often, it's because they tapped into a value. Maybe the part of writing your bestseller that you loved most was *connecting* with readers (value: connection or service). That might guide you to make your next goal something like hosting intimate workshops or starting a podcast to engage in dialogue with others, rather than, say, locking yourself away to write an even bigger book just for the sake of outdoing the last. Or if you cherish *independence*, perhaps the best part of your career triumph was the autonomy you gained – in which case, your next pursuit should preserve your freedom rather than bind you to a rigid structure, even if it's prestigious.

In sum, think of a new goal as a bridge between your present self and your ideal life, built on pillars of your values. Every plank of that bridge should feel connected to what you hold dear. When you walk that bridge – pursue that goal – each step will feel purposeful. Instead of chasing validation, you'll be *living* your values day by day. This transforms the pursuit itself into a source of satisfaction. The award at the end, if there is one, is just icing on the cake. The true reward is that you spent your time and energy on something that matters. Value-driven goals ensure that "success" is no longer defined by others or by abstract standards, but by how authentically you can live out what is most important to you.

Start Small, Start Playfully: Finding Joy in "Mini Summits"

After a big achievement, you might feel pressure for your next step to be something *equally big*. It's as if people expect you to announce another grand quest immediately – and maybe you expect that of yourself, too. But here's a liberating truth: not every next step has to be a colossal mission. In fact, especially as you recover from the last climb, it can be incredibly refreshing and wise to start small. Think of this phase as an open field for playful experimentation, not a make-or-break test of your worth. You've earned some breathing room. This is the time to explore, to try on new roles or activities like trying on different hats, and see what brings a genuine smile to your face.

Why start small? For one, taking on a massive goal right away can be overwhelming and even counterproductive. Diving headlong into a new project of epic scale might simply replicate the stress and pressure you just left behind. It could also be a way of avoiding the emotional processing of your last achievement – a sort of rebound goal that might not actually suit you, as we discussed earlier. By contrast, small goals or projects come with lower stakes and greater flexibility. You can dip a toe into a new endeavor without feeling like you're betting your entire identity on it. This frees you to rediscover the joy of learning and growing, without the weight of huge expectations.

Consider a top executive who retires or steps down after decades of nonstop work. Suddenly, their calendar is empty, and that can be terrifying. One approach would be to immediately try to fill it with another full-time commitment – perhaps joining multiple boards or starting a new enterprise – essentially jumping back on the same hamster wheel. But another approach, a playful one, would be to experiment with a bunch of small activities: audit a course at the local university, volunteer once a week at a community kitchen, take up photography on the weekends, join a weekly tennis group. None of these things individually is life-defining or grand. Yet each is a "mini summit" of its own – a small challenge or new terrain to explore. Our executive might discover that the photography class rekindles a long-lost artistic streak, or that volunteering brings a sense of fulfillment he hadn't felt in years. If something doesn't click, no big deal – he can pivot to another activity. The low stakes of starting small mean there's no devastating failure if a particular interest doesn't pan out; it's all part of the adventure.

Starting playfully also helps rebuild something crucial that might have gotten lost in your intense pursuit of success: *a sense of curiosity*. When we were children, we learned and accomplished things in a spirit of play all the time. We weren't keeping score or plotting five-year plans as we learned to ride a bike or draw with crayons – we just tried things because they looked fun or interesting. As adults, especially high-achieving adults, we often lose that lightness. We tend to approach goals with a very serious, all-or-nothing mentality. But after a major accomplishment (and the sobering realization that even that didn't "fix" life forever), you have a golden opportunity to reclaim a beginner's mindset. Give yourself permission to be a novice at something again, to be a kid in a sandbox trying new toys. Sign up for a short workshop in a field you know nothing about, just because it intrigues you. Allow yourself to be clumsy, to ask questions, even to fail in small, consequence-free ways. You might be surprised at how much *fun* it is to not be the expert for a change. And fun is far from frivolous – it can be deeply healing and energizing.

For example, one former Fortune 500 CEO we know started taking improv comedy classes after he left his role. It was a completely different world from corporate strategy meetings – in improv, the whole point was to *not* have a plan, to react in the moment, and to laugh at mistakes. At first, he felt ridiculous and well out of his comfort zone (imagine a buttoned-up executive pretending to be a talking shrimp in an improv sketch!). But that weekly class became the highlight of his schedule. It allowed him to tap into creativity and spontaneity he didn't realize he had, and it taught him to enjoy the process without any concern for outcome. "There's no winning in improv," he later reflected, "you just play. I hadn't 'just played' in decades." That playful small step opened up new facets of his personality. It didn't turn him into a professional comedian, nor was that the goal – the goal was simply to explore and to reignite his zest for life.

Starting small can also mean short-term projects instead of long-term commitments. If you're considering a big change but aren't sure, try a pilot version of it. Interested in a career switch? Rather than quitting your current position and leaping blindly, perhaps take on a short consulting assignment or a freelance project in that new field to taste what it's like. Thinking about writing a book? Start with a blog or a series of essays to develop your voice and see if the subject truly engages you beyond a fleeting infatuation. Want to improve your fitness but feeling intimidated? Set a 30-day challenge to walk 10,000 steps every day, or join a low-key local 5K run before deciding if a marathon is in your future. These bite-sized goals can build confidence and clarity. Each one you complete gives you feedback about yourself: *Did I enjoy this? Did it make me feel more alive?* If yes, go a little further down that path. If not, you've lost nothing – you gained experience and can course-correct.

A playful, experimental mindset also reduces the fear of failure that often paralyzes achievers at the top. When all your previous moves have been successful, it's easy to become risk-averse, thinking *"What if I try this new thing and I'm terrible at it? What if I embarrass myself?"* But by framing your next steps as experiments, you grant yourself grace. You're not failing; you're learning. Thomas Edison famously said, after numerous prototypes of the lightbulb, "I haven't failed, I've just found 10,000 ways that won't work." In your case, trying a handful of new hobbies or mini-goals isn't a matter of success or failure at all – it's about discovery. You might discover an unexpected passion, or you might discover that something you thought you'd love actually doesn't suit you. Both outcomes are equally valuable data for designing a more fulfilling life.

Another benefit of starting small and playfully is that it keeps you engaged *during* a period of transition without overwhelming you. Many high achievers fall into a deep lull right after their big win – they go from 100 miles an hour to a dead stop. That abrupt halt can worsen feelings of emptiness. Small goals act like gentle forward momentum. They give you a reason to get out of bed in the morning (even if it's just "I need to water my new garden seedlings" or "I have guitar class today and I want to practice a bit before") without the crushing weight of a huge new responsibility. Psychologically, this is much healthier than either stagnating or overloading yourself. Think of it as keeping your engine humming without immediately flooring the accelerator. You stay in motion, but you're free to change directions, slow down, or speed up as you wish.

Lastly, remember to savor the *play* in this approach. If one of your mini summits is, say, learning to cook French pastries, let yourself be delightfully absorbed in it. Laugh at the grotesque croissant that comes out of the oven the first time. Invite friends to taste-test your experimental creations and make an evening of it. The point is not to turn every hobby into another arena of perfectionism (resist that temptation!); the point is to enjoy being a beginner and to reconnect with the part of you that thrives on curiosity and newness. In doing so, you're actually rebuilding an internal resource that will serve you well for any larger goals to come: a resilient, enthusiastic spirit that remembers how to find happiness in the process, not just in the end result.

Embrace the Journey: Continuous Growth Over One Final Destination

If there's one lesson that echoes throughout this book, it's that fulfillment comes not from a single achievement, but from the ongoing journey of growth. Now that you're looking to the future beyond your big win, it's essential to embrace this truth more than ever. Life after a summit isn't about identifying one ultimate goal to top everything you've done before – it's about opening yourself to continual discovery and purpose. Rather than a peak that ends the story, think of your life as a series of chapters, each with its own quests, lessons, and rewards. In other words, *the journey itself is where meaning lives.*

Experts in psychology and human development note that maintaining a sense of meaning along with a healthy dose of novelty in life is a key ingredient to long-term satisfaction. Why novelty? Because our minds and spirits thrive on growth and change. If you were to simply rest on your laurels permanently, life would soon feel stagnant. Humans are curious creatures; we're wired to seek out new challenges, to learn, to evolve. Novelty doesn't mean chasing thrill for thrill's sake – it means ensuring that as years go by, you continue to have fresh experiences, meet new ideas, and face different kinds of challenges that keep you engaged. It could be as simple as exploring new places (traveling to countries you've never been, or even taking different routes through your own city), or as profound as developing new relationships and roles (like becoming a mentor, a parent, or a student again in some field). This infusion of the new prevents life from shrinking. It keeps your world expanding, even after you've ticked off many of the classic boxes of success.

Hand in hand with novelty is meaning. Novel experiences by themselves can be fun, but for deep satisfaction, we crave meaning – a sense that our actions matter in the grand scheme of things, or at least in the lives of others. This is where purpose comes in. Embracing the journey means recognizing that purpose is not a finish line, but an ever-evolving target. You create and discover meaning through the *process* of living aligned with your values and pursuing what excites you, as we've discussed. In practical terms, this could mean that instead of saying "I must achieve X, and then I'll have lasting fulfillment," you say "I want to live each day in a way that is meaningful to me, and *that* is fulfillment." Your goals then become stepping stones or vehicles for that meaningful daily life, not merely end points.

Let's revisit the metaphor of a mountain climber one more time. Imagine that reaching your big achievement was like summiting a towering peak. Coming down from it, you face a vast landscape dotted with many mountains, valleys, rivers, and forests. Some peaks are taller than the one you climbed, many are smaller, and some adventures lie not on mountains at all but perhaps at sea level or below the earth in caves. Embracing the journey means you don't feel compelled to only go for the next higher peak in a linear, competitive fashion. Instead, you appreciate that there are many meaningful paths open to you. You might choose to climb a smaller mountain next, not because it's higher, but because perhaps it's more beautiful or has a trail that interests you. Or you might trek through the forest for a while to enjoy the calm shade and learn about the ecosystem there. You could venture to the ocean to learn to sail, a completely different skill than mountaineering. Each of these journeys will teach you something and contribute to your growth. Each will have its own challenges and rewards. There's no rule that life must be an endless ascent to ever-greater heights; it can be an exploration outward in breadth and inward in depth.

Many accomplished people find their greatest fulfillment in later chapters of life not from exceeding their past accomplishments, but from expanding into new roles that give them a renewed sense of purpose. A CEO becomes a mentor to young startups and finds joy in their protégés' successes. A world-class athlete retires from competition and discovers a calling in coaching, guiding others to achieve their dreams, or in advocating for mental health in sports. A famous artist might shift from creating art to curating exhibitions that uplift emerging voices, or to teaching workshops that ignite creativity in others. These paths might not come with the same glory or adrenaline as the original achievements, but they offer something deeper: a legacy of meaning, connection, and contribution. And importantly, they keep the individual engaged in growth. As a mentor or coach or teacher, you learn and evolve too – often in unexpected and deeply satisfying ways. You remain a traveler on the road of life, not a static figure framed only by past trophies.

Scientific research underscores the importance of this mindset. One study found that people who continually seek out new and diverse experiences tend to report higher happiness and even show more activity in brain regions associated with reward and curiosity. In other words, *variety and exploration feed our emotional well-being.* Other studies in positive psychology have noted that having an ongoing sense of purpose (which can be as simple as having something to look forward to and work toward) is linked to better life satisfaction, health, and even longevity. In fact, in Blue Zones – regions of the world where people frequently live past 100 years old in good health – one common factor is that these individuals have a reason to get up in the morning, whether it's tending their garden, caring for grandchildren, or volunteering in the community. They never "retire" from having meaningful engagement with life. The Japanese concept of ikigai speaks to this: it's the idea of a life purpose or passion that fuels you. Those centenarians might consider their daily walk to fish or their ritual of writing poetry as their "goals," modest though they seem – but these activities imbue their days with purpose and pleasure. The same principle applies no matter your stage of life or level of past success.

So, as you set out on your new goals, remind yourself that the journey is the destination. If you decide to run that marathon, of course the day of the race will be a proud moment – but the true value will lie in the months of training, the discipline you cultivate on early morning runs, the camaraderie with others you meet on the trail, the way you gradually push past what you thought were your limits. If your next chapter is launching a new business or initiative, by all means dream of the launch party and the moment you open the doors – but know that your real life will be in the day-to-day creative problem-solving, the connections you build with your new team or clients, the small victories and lessons learned as you grow the venture. When you embrace the journey, you allow yourself to find happiness and meaning every step of the way, not just at the end.

There's an old adage often told to those who climb literal mountains: "You cannot stay on the summit forever; you have to come down eventually." It's on the way down, and on to other trails, that the rest of life unfolds. Coming down from a summit doesn't diminish your accomplishment; it simply means it's time for new vistas. The beauty of life after achieving a big goal is that it can be an *open road*. Rather than a daunting blank page where you must write something earth-shattering to top your last chapter, think of it as a road stretching out with many forks. Each fork represents a choice or opportunity – some big, some small. You get to choose which paths to explore. Some will lead to new high peaks; others might lead you through quiet, lovely meadows of experience. There is no single "right" path, only the path *you choose* and commit to making meaningful.

As you walk this open road, stay receptive to surprise and serendipity. Not all goals need to be set in stone; sometimes life presents you with an unexpected opportunity that wasn't on your original map but turns out to be incredibly fulfilling. By embracing the journey, you won't be blinded by tunnel vision for one outcome – you'll be able to recognize and seize these moments. Perhaps while pursuing a small goal, you stumble onto a passion that becomes a larger calling. Perhaps through mentoring someone, you discover a new business idea that excites you more than anything you've done. Embracing a journey mindset means you are continuously *iterating* your purpose. It's a living thing, not a one-time mission.

In practical terms, how do you keep embracing the journey day by day? It can be as simple as periodically asking yourself: *What am I learning right now? How am I growing?* Even if your current project is difficult or progress is slow, if you can identify what you're learning or how it's shaping you, you'll feel a sense of forward motion. Also, take time to celebrate small milestones along the way. Don't wait for the big finale to acknowledge your efforts. That could mean journaling weekly about achievements and insights, or sharing updates with a friend or mentor who appreciates your process. By honoring the journey in this way, you reinforce that your life is rich *today*, not just someday in the future.

Finally, remember that your journey doesn't have to be a solo trek. Finding purpose often involves connecting with others – whether as collaborators, students, teachers, beneficiaries, or fellow travelers. Many executives and achievers find renewed meaning in *community*: joining a peer group of others in a similar transition, engaging in community service, or simply nurturing personal relationships that may have been sidelined. These human connections are part of the meaningful path. They remind you that life is not just about climbing ladders, but about walking together. As you embrace continuous growth, also embrace the people and communities around you. Success voids tend to shrink when you're sharing your journey and contributing to something beyond yourself.

In embracing the journey, you are effectively saying: My life is not defined by one peak, but by the many experiences, values, and purposes I weave together over time. This perspective transforms the future from a scary unknown – a blank page – into an exciting adventure – an open road. Instead of fearing that your best days are behind you, you come to see that there are many best days yet to come, each in different flavors. There will be new summits, yes, but also plateaus where you can rest and reflect, and valleys that might challenge you in new ways and make you stronger. All of it is valuable. All of it is life.

As we conclude this chapter, take a moment to look ahead in your mind's eye. The summit of your great achievement is behind you, visible in the distance as a proud memory. Ahead lies a landscape of possibility. A new vision shaped by your authentic self-beckons. A handful of meaningful goals aligned with your values light the path like guiding stars. You carry a playful spirit in your backpack, ready to try new things without fear. And you carry the wisdom that the road itself – winding and unpredictable as it may be – is where you will find fulfillment. With that wisdom, step forward. Your next adventure awaits, and it's going to be remarkable in its own unique way. The success you've had was not an ending, but a beginning of a more conscious, purpose-driven journey. Embrace it with open arms, and you'll find that meaning and happiness are not peaks to conquer, but companions that walk beside you mile after mile.

Chapter 9

From Isolation to Inspiration – Support and Contribution

Share Your Feelings

It's hard to admit when you're struggling, especially after you've achieved something most people only dream about. You might think, "I should be on top of the world, so why do I feel so low?" This disconnect between outward success and inner turmoil can be deeply isolating. In reality, post-achievement letdowns are surprisingly common – even among elite performers. Olympic champion Michael Phelps revealed that after reaching his lifelong goals, he felt a "traumatic emptiness". He has observed that this post-Olympic crash is actually common among other elite athletes. Such stories show that no matter how brilliant your victory, you're not the only one who has felt hollow once the applause fades. Recognizing this is the first step to breaking out of your bubble of silence.

The next step is daring to share your feelings with someone you trust. It might feel uncomfortable to confess, "I'm actually struggling after my big success," but speaking that truth out loud can be profoundly freeing. When Phelps finally opened up about his depression, he said *"opening up took a huge weight off my back. It made life easier."* Likewise, countless people have found relief in simply telling a friend or loved one about their post-achievement slump. Studies back this up: simply talking about your emotions helps relieve negative feelings, literally changing how your brain processes distress. In other words, voicing what you're going through can start to take away some of the feelings' power over you.

Opening up often invites empathy and understanding in return. You might fear others won't "get it" – *How can I complain when I've accomplished so much?* – but you may be surprised. True friends or close colleagues are likely to respond with care, not judgment. Many have quietly faced similar emotional lows in their own lives and can relate more than you think. By breaking the ice, you might even give them permission to share their experiences too, turning a lonely struggle into a shared human moment. Engaging in discussions with others who have encountered similar feelings shines light on how normal post-achievement blues really are, offering you validation and a sense of commonality. Simply hearing "I've been there too" from a peer or mentor can make you feel far less alone and abnormal.

If you're not ready to open up to people you know, consider speaking with a professional counselor or joining a support group. There is zero shame in this – on the contrary, it's a wise and courageous step when emotions run intense. A therapist or support group provides a safe, confidential space to unload what you're carrying. Sometimes just saying the words "I'm not okay right now" to a compassionate listener is enough to release months (or years) of pent-up stress. As one mental health expert put it: *"You don't have to carry this alone."* Talking about your feelings "makes a huge difference." You might also gain new insights as you hear yourself explain what you feel. What's crucial is remembering that you are allowed to seek support. Just because you "made it" doesn't mean you lost the right to feel bad or to ask for help.

By sharing your feelings, you chip away at the power they have over you. The isolation begins to crack. Picture a pressure valve finally releasing – the build-up of confusion, guilt, and sadness starts to escape. You may literally feel lighter, as Phelps did, after confiding in someone. And far from thinking less of you, true friends and mentors will likely admire your honesty and offer support. In fact, vulnerability often deepens relationships. By being open, you allow others to walk alongside you in the aftermath, rather than you struggling on your own. Bit by bit, openness replaces isolation with relief and turns loneliness into feeling understood.

Find Your Tribe

Opening up to one trusted person is powerful; connecting with a community of peers who truly understand your journey can be life-changing. After a big achievement, you might feel like an outlier among your usual circle. Your old friends, loving as they are, might not grasp why you feel empty after getting that promotion or publishing that book. This is where finding *your tribe* comes in – the people who "get it" because they've been on a similar climb and experienced that same strange void at the top.

Consider seeking out peers in your field or others who have navigated "life after success." When you surround yourself with those who have walked a parallel path, you quickly realize your feelings are normal, not a personal flaw. For example, entrepreneurs often join mastermind circles or networks to share the unique struggles that come with business success. High-level leaders have their own forums as well – one survey of CEOs found that almost half reported feeling lonely in their role, and most believed this isolation negatively impacted their performance. That's why organizations like the Young Presidents' Organization (YPO) exist – to provide a platform for chief executives to engage candidly with peers around the world. In a similar way, whatever your arena – sports, arts, tech, academia – connecting with *fellow "after the summit" travelers* gives you a safe space to swap stories and strategies with people who understand.

Finding your tribe might involve joining an existing community or creating your own. You could look for meet-ups, online forums, or peer support groups related to your profession or passions. Networks exist in nearly every arena – retired athletes, creative professionals, academics – where people share how they navigated the "now what?" feeling after a major milestone. These communities remind you that *you are not weird or ungrateful* for feeling a void – it's a shared human experience among high achievers. As one leadership coach noted, even the most successful people need an environment where they can be vulnerable and learn in a safe, trusting space.

Even if no formal group exists, a few honest conversations can spark your own tribe. Invite a fellow achiever for a coffee chat and share what you're going through — you may get a relieved *"You feel that way too? I thought it was just me!"* in response. In that moment of mutual understanding, a powerful connection is formed. Over time, such relationships can grow into a trusted support network that you lean on for advice, encouragement, and perspective. Engaging with a supportive peer network can dissolve the isolation that often follows big success. In fact, members of peer advisory groups frequently report that being part of such a group helps them overcome loneliness and boosts their confidence going forward.

Beyond emotional support, your tribe offers practical insight for redefining life after achievement. You can swap strategies: How did they find new goals or balance after their peak moment? How do they handle the expectations that others (or they themselves) now have? The collective wisdom in these conversations sparks ideas for your own next chapter. For example, one person in your circle might share how volunteering in the community gave them a renewed sense of purpose, while another found that starting a fun side project reignited their excitement. Their stories prove that there is life – and purpose – beyond the pinnacle you reached. Surrounded by understanding peers, your road ahead starts to look broader and more hopeful, illuminated by others' experiences.

Belonging to a group of like-minded achievers can also restore a sense of *camaraderie* and fun that might be missing from your life lately. The moments of laughter and camaraderie you find in such groups are therapeutic. They reconnect you to the human side of your journey – the shared struggles and little victories – rather than solely the shiny trophy at the end. In a tribe, you're not "the award-winner" being put on a pedestal; you're just you, a fellow traveler among friends.

Ultimately, finding your tribe replaces alienation with belonging. Your regular social circle may love you, but they might not fully grasp the success hangover you're experiencing. Your tribe does. Within that community, your story will resonate, your feelings will be validated, and your evolving identity will be supported. The perspective you gain from peers can truly transform your mindset. What once felt like the end of the road ("I achieved my goal… now what?") begins to look like a new beginning – one that many others have navigated successfully and can help guide you through. With your tribe by your side, you start to see beyond the summit and into the next chapter of life that lies ahead.

From Success to Significance

After scaling a personal Everest, it's common to ask, "What now?" When the celebrations are over, you may sense that chasing the next high-profile goal won't cure the emptiness. This is where a profound shift can occur: moving from success to significance. In simple terms, that means turning your focus outward – using your talents, experience, and hard-won wisdom to help others climb their mountains. Filling the void isn't about accumulating another accolade; it's about finding purpose beyond your own accomplishments. Many high achievers discover that the antidote to the post-success void is to transform success into service.

One powerful way to do this is through mentorship. By coaching or guiding someone else, you convert your experience into fuel for another person's journey. For example, a retired executive might mentor a young startup founder, or a former star athlete might coach kids in the sport. Suddenly, your story – with all its triumphs and mistakes – becomes a roadmap for someone else. The beauty is that this process uplifts both parties. The mentee gains wisdom and encouragement, while the mentor often experiences a renewed sense of meaning. Research confirms that mentoring isn't just beneficial for the mentee; it can boost the mentor's well-being too. Serving as a mentor provides meaningful social connection, higher self-esteem, and a fresh sense of purpose for the mentor, all of which help combat the isolation that may follow a big win. In essence, helping others grow reminds you that your journey matters *beyond* the trophy on your shelf.

Volunteering and community service are another avenue for turning success into significance. When you step outside your individual achievements and contribute to a cause, it completely reframes your perspective. You realize that your skills and success can be tools for good. Perhaps you volunteer your expertise to a nonprofit, or you spend a few hours a week supporting a community project. Not only do others benefit, but so do you. Studies have found that volunteering is great for mental health – it can *lower stress, reduce depression and anxiety, and boost overall life satisfaction*. Beyond these benefits, giving back instills a deeper sense of purpose. Focusing on what you can give – rather than what you get – often leads to a more lasting contentment.

Think about the concept of legacy. Achievements, no matter how grand, can feel fleeting once attained, but the impact you have on others tends to endure. Take the story of Dean Niewolny. By his early 40s,

Niewolny had everything he thought he wanted – a top executive title, wealth, luxury toys – yet he felt empty inside. He reevaluated his life and decided to channel his energy into giving back. He and his wife even sold some of their luxuries to help start an orphanage in South Africa. "So much joy came out of that," Niewolny said, reflecting on how taking the focus off himself and helping others brought him *incredible joy and balance*. His story illustrates a universal truth: when we use our success to lift others up, we often find a level of fulfillment that no trophy or bonus could ever provide.

There's science to back this up. Psychologists have found that *meaningful activities* – things that use your skills while also making a positive difference for others – significantly boost overall happiness. Meanwhile, beyond a certain point, more wealth or accolades don't increase happiness. Once you've achieved enough for yourself, the next leap in life satisfaction comes from contributing to others. When we use our success to serve something larger than ourselves, our own happiness meter rises again. Generosity and purpose answer the nagging post-victory question of "What now?" with a clear mission: to make an impact.

Moving from success to significance can take many forms, big or small. You don't have to launch a charity or donate millions (though if you're in a position to, that's wonderful). It can be as personal as being a reliable mentor to a handful of younger people in your field, or as local as volunteering at a school or community center. It might mean using your platform to draw attention to an issue you care about. What matters is that you're channeling your experience into contribution. In doing so, you'll likely find that the emptiness starts to fill with new energy. Helping someone else climb their mountain rekindles your own passion. You start to see that your value isn't just in what you achieved *then* (in the past), but in what you are doing *now* for others.

Many people report that by turning to service, they regain a sense of identity and excitement. For instance, a former athlete coaching a youth team can feel the thrill of the sport return. In lifting others, we inadvertently lift ourselves. The success void becomes a source of meaning, even inspiration, as you witness the ripple effects of your contribution. You realize that your summit was never just yours; it can become part of someone else's journey upward too. This recognition can fundamentally rebuild your identity. You evolve from "the one who succeeded" into "the one who helps others succeed." That is a powerful, purpose-driven identity that outlasts any single accomplishment.

Story – The Mentor's New Mission

Lisa sat in her home office, staring at the walls lined with awards from her crowning achievement. At 38, she had become the youngest partner at her firm – a goal she'd pursued for nearly two decades. Colleagues toasted her promotion and her family beamed with pride. Yet in the weeks after the celebration, Lisa felt an unexpected hollowness. Each morning she woke up thinking, *What do I do now?* The work that once excited her felt oddly routine. For the first time in her career, she even found herself dreading Monday mornings.

At first, Lisa kept these feelings to herself. On paper, her life was perfect; admitting her discontent felt ungrateful. So she soldiered on, wearing a polite smile at the office while a fog of purposelessness settled over her. Her husband noticed her restlessness and gently asked if she was okay. *"Just tired,"* she replied, never confessing the worry that gnawed at her: *Why aren't I happy? What's wrong with me?*

Everything began to change one Saturday when Lisa attended a local college alumni event as a volunteer speaker. She had agreed to host a roundtable for young women starting their careers – a simple mentoring session. She nearly canceled that morning, questioning what value she could offer in her current funk. But she went anyway. Seated at a small table with a half-dozen recent graduates, Lisa started sharing the story of her career: the hard lessons, the mistakes, the victories. She spoke candidly about the self-doubt she had battled along the way. To her surprise, the students hung on every word. When Lisa admitted she once almost quit her job early on because she felt like an imposter, several heads nodded and one young woman sighed with relief, *"I'm so glad to know someone like you went through that."* At that moment, a spark flickered in Lisa. What she had seen as her private burden was actually *helping* these aspiring professionals.

After the roundtable, one of the students, Maya, shyly approached Lisa. *"I learned so much from you today,"* Maya said. *"Would you maybe be willing to grab coffee sometime? I'd love to keep in touch."* In that instant, Lisa felt a small rush of purpose – a feeling that had been absent for months. *"Of course,"* she replied warmly. That one coffee chat turned into monthly meet-ups, which soon evolved into a more formal mentoring relationship. As Lisa got to know Maya, she found herself growing deeply invested in the younger woman's progress. They practiced interview skills and discussed career dilemmas; Lisa even helped Maya weigh different job offers. All the experience Lisa had accumulated over years of hard work – experience that had been lying dormant during her post-promotion slump – was now being put to use to fuel someone else's growth.

Over the next few months, a visible transformation took root in Lisa. She still gave her all at work, but now she had a *new spark* in her life: those mentoring sessions with Maya (and soon with two other mentees Maya introduced). Lisa genuinely looked forward to their weekly calls. She listened to their anxieties about work and life, and she shared her own stories and advice. In these conversations, she felt a surge of energy and joy that had been missing since her big promotion. After each call, she would hang up with a smile on her face. One evening, her husband noticed this and said, *"You seem happier lately."* Lisa paused, realizing he was right. *"I am,"* she replied, and the smile that accompanied her words was genuine.

By coaching others, Lisa discovered that her journey held value beyond the accolades. When Maya aced a job interview using techniques they had practiced, Lisa felt as proud as if it were her own victory. She found herself cheering on each of her mentees' wins – celebrating when one got a promotion, brainstorming solutions when another hit a stumbling block. And each time, she experienced a sense of fulfillment deeper than any award or bonus had ever given her. The emptiness that once followed her big achievement was gradually filling with a new sense of mission. Lisa's laughter and enthusiasm returned at work, and even her coworkers noticed her uplifted mood. She knew this renewal wasn't due to a change in diet or a vacation – it was coming from within, sparked by the meaning she was finding in helping others.

One year later, Lisa returned to the same alumni event – this time with Maya as a co-panelist by her side. She watched with pride as Maya confidently led part of the discussion, something the shy recent graduate of a year ago would never have done. In that moment, Lisa realized that this was the true legacy of her success. Not a plaque on a wall, but a living impact on another person's life. Her summit had become the foundation for someone else's climb. Lisa understood now that reaching her goal was only the beginning of a longer, richer journey. By moving from isolation to inspiration – by seeking support and then giving back – she had tapped into a well of purpose that no trophy could ever provide. Helping others had healed her own void, and it created a ripple of growth and positivity that would outlast any single accomplishment.

Chapter 10

Beyond the Finish Line – Redefining Success and Moving Forward

Success, Redefined

Standing at the finish line of a long-fought journey, you might expect to feel complete. Yet many high achievers have discovered that reaching the summit of success can leave them unexpectedly hollow inside. This realization is a catalyst to redefine what success truly means. No longer is *success* defined solely by standing on a podium or hitting a sales number. Instead, it comes from living in alignment with your deepest values, experiencing genuine joy and growth, and feeling at peace with yourself in everyday life. In a world increasingly aware of burnout and mental health, there has been a seismic shift in how we view success: emotional well-being and inner fulfillment are emerging as more meaningful benchmarks than wealth or status. In short, *real success* is about *who you are* and *how you live*, not just what you've accomplished on paper.

It's easy to chase society's ready-made checklist of achievements – the promotion, the award, the financial milestone – only to find that ticking those boxes doesn't guarantee happiness. Psychologists even have a term for this false promise of happiness at the end of a goal: the "arrival fallacy," which is the illusion that achieving a significant goal will bring lasting bliss when in fact the satisfaction is often fleeting. We tell ourselves *"I'll be happy when I get there."* But how many times have we all gotten *"there"* and wondered, *"Is this it?"* Consider the stark examples: Nearly 80% of Olympic athletes experience a depressive slump after the Games, and countless executives feel oddly empty after a big career win. Even a legendary sports champion, upon finally clinching a long-coveted title, was found weeping in the locker room, saying, *"I gave my whole life for this, but it feels so empty."* These stories, from Olympians and CEOs alike, highlight a profound lesson: external accolades alone cannot sustain us. They are moments in time, not life's full meaning.

So what is the alternative? Success must be redefined on your own terms. This means choosing goals and values based on what genuinely fulfills you, rather than what impresses others. Research suggests that true success is found in authenticity – aligning your life with your personal values and inner truths. You might decide that success now means having a calm morning routine and time with family, rather than a new job title. It could mean pursuing a passion project that pays little but enriches your soul. It might even be as simple as ending each day feeling content with how you treated people and yourself. One psychology expert put it succinctly: we can all choose to define success for ourselves and create a life that feels *authentic* and *value-aligned.* When you shift your focus to inner fulfillment over external validation, you break the cycle of the arrival fallacy and find that success is not a one-time finish line at all – it's a continuous, personal journey.

To embrace this new definition, pause and reflect on what truly matters to you. Perhaps it's the *quality of your relationships*, the *balance* in your day-to-day life, or the feeling that you're contributing to something meaningful. These are not the kind of milestones that get announced in a press release, but they have a profound impact on your happiness. In fact, an extensive Harvard study on adult development found that strong relationships, not material wealth, are the single greatest predictor of long-term health and satisfaction. Knowing this, ask yourself: *If your traditional success doesn't support your well-being or align with your values, is it truly success?* By redefining success now to include inner peace, purpose, and joy, you ensure that *making it* will no longer leave you empty. Instead, every achievement – big or small – will be in service of a life that genuinely feels successful from within.

Life Is a Journey, Not a Destination

When you recognize that success is personal and internal, a liberating truth emerges: life is a continuous journey, not a one-time destination. There is no final peak where everything is "solved" forever – and that's not a drawback, it's a beautiful reality. The end of one accomplishment is not *the end of your story*; it's merely the turning of a page, the start of the next chapter. In this way, life after "making it" can be as rich and meaningful as all the years you spent striving – perhaps even more so, once you release the pressure to have one climactic finale. Remember the old adage: *"It's not the destination that counts; it's the journey."* Every goal you pursue and every peak you climb is part of a greater expedition, one filled with valleys and vistas, twists and turns.

Think of a mountain climber who has reached the summit she dreamt of for years. As she stands at the top, she realizes the horizon stretches out to new mountains beyond. Rather than a dead-end, the summit offers a broader view of what else is possible. Life is very much like that. Each time you scale one mountain, you gain the perspective to see other peaks you hadn't noticed before. There is always more to explore, learn, and experience. This realization takes the pressure off any single achievement being the make-or-break moment. There is no "final" peak; there are many peaks, with valleys of rest and growth in between. By viewing life as a series of adventures instead of one ultimate conquest, you allow yourself to appreciate the journey itself. The process – with all its ups and downs – becomes the point, not just the medals or milestones at the end.

Adopting this mindset can be profoundly relieving. If you've ever thought "Will I ever top that big success?" the answer might be: *maybe not in the same way – but you don't need to.* Fulfillment is not a one-time prize to clutch. It's the day-to-day sense of engagement and purpose you get from continuing to grow. Indeed, psychological research on motivation shows that humans are hardwired to thrive in pursuit of meaningful goals, and the joy often comes more from *striving* than from reaching the end-point. We actually *need* that sense of pursuit; when it vanishes after an accomplishment, it's natural to feel a void. The key is to recognize this pattern and embrace the idea that the journey must go on. As one observer noted, *happiness routinely lies in the journey itself – in the relationships we build and in the moments of growth and self-discovery along the way.*

Consider your own life as a book composed of many chapters rather than a single climax. You may have just finished an exhilarating chapter where you achieved something great. Now a new chapter awaits, and it can be just as engaging as the last. There will be new characters to meet, new lessons to learn, perhaps new challenges to overcome – and that is okay. In fact, that is wonderful. Because when life is a journey, you always have room to evolve. You can cherish past successes for what they were – important chapters in your story – without expecting them to permanently fulfill you. The next chapters might take you in unexpected directions, and that openness is what makes life exciting. By understanding that fulfillment comes from continuously moving forward (and sometimes sideways), you free yourself from the illusion that you must cling to one peak or one moment. The road ahead is open, and knowing that *there is no finish line to a life well-lived* can fill you with optimism and curiosity about the future.

Wholeness Over Achievement

After redefining success and embracing the journey, an important shift occurs: you begin to value wholeness and well-being over sheer achievement. In our accomplishment-obsessed culture, we often applaud the person who sacrifices everything for a goal – their sleep, their health, their relationships. But what if true success is something more *holistic?* Imagine measuring success not just by what you've achieved, but by how healthy and whole you are in the process. This means that your mental health, emotional richness, and personal growth are just as important as the next award or metric on your resume – if not more important. In practical terms, this could mean celebrating the fact that you maintained balance during a tough project, or that you managed stress with grace, or kept your values intact under pressure. Those are victories too, and they're deeply meaningful ones.

A growing body of evidence – and a growing chorus of voices in society – supports this holistic view. We know that money and status alone don't equal happiness; studies and long-term observations have shown that factors like mental well-being and relationships play a far greater role in life satisfaction. As mentioned earlier, the longest-running Harvard study found that strong relationships are the clearest predictor of a happy, healthy life. Similarly, many high performers learn the hard way that neglecting self-care and relationships can strip the joy from even the greatest achievements. Think of the corporate executive who burned out chasing quarterly targets, or the superstar athlete who sacrificed their mental health for gold medals. Ultimately, such "success" rings hollow if it comes at the cost of one's wholeness. As one leadership writer observed, relationships influence our sense of worth far more than medals or money ever will. In other words, a balanced dinner with loved ones might contribute more to your long-term fulfillment than an extra zero in your bank account or a trophy on the shelf.

Prioritizing wholeness means recognizing the validity of every dimension of success. Have you taken care of your mind and body? That's success. Have you continued to learn and grow as a person? That's success. Did you stay true to your principles when tested, or make time for the people you care about? Those are huge successes. When you expand your definition of winning this way, you give yourself permission to be a whole human being instead of a single-minded achievement machine. You might start to set goals like maintaining a morning meditation practice for a month, or improving your work-life harmony, treating them as equally worthy of celebration as any professional milestone. Emotional well-being and personal growth become integral parts of the equation of success, not afterthoughts. For example, practicing mindfulness or gratitude regularly can be a triumph in living well; nurturing a friendship through honest conversation can be as important an accomplishment as any business deal.

Crucially, focusing on wholeness helps ensure you *never lose yourself* in pursuit of a goal again. By keeping your mental and emotional health in focus, you create a safety net against the tunnel vision that led to the "success void" in the first place. This holistic approach acts like an inner compass: if chasing a new goal starts to break your peace or violate your values, the compass signals that something is off. You can then recalibrate, rather than blindly pushing forward into burnout or disillusionment. In practical terms, this might mean turning down a promotion that promises more pay but would destroy your family time, or deciding that *this year's success* will be defined by how much you grow and learn rather than how much you win. By valuing well-being as much as achievement, you set yourself up for sustainable success – the kind that enriches your life rather than consumes it. This way, each accomplishment you pursue will be in harmony with your overall happiness. You'll be succeeding *as a whole person*, not just a high performer. And that is a success that lasts.

From Void to Vision

In the aftermath of reaching a pinnacle and feeling the void, it's easy to see that emptiness as a negative – a scary blank space where your driving purpose used to be. But what if that very void is actually a blank canvas, waiting for you to paint a new vision of your life? The end of one journey gives you a rare gift: a moment of clarity to ask, *"What now?"* rather than simply racing on a treadmill of goals set by others. This final section is a call-to-arms to use the experience of the "success void" as fuel to craft a richer, more meaningful life going forward. The confusion, the questions, and yes, even the discomfort you felt after your big win can all become catalysts for positive change – if you choose to see them that way.

Consider the perspective shift that happens when you view your accomplishments *"not as a letdown, but as a boost to finding more meaning and purpose"* in your life. In other words, the fact that your achievement didn't fulfill you forever isn't a sign that something's wrong with you or with the achievement – it's information. It's telling you that you are ready for something *more*, something different, something deeper. Many people who have gone through this realize that their big win was actually a springboard into a new chapter of personal growth. For example, an entrepreneur might sell their company and initially feel empty, but that void pushes them to discover a new passion for mentoring young innovators. An Olympic champion, after the post-Games blues, might channel their energy into advocating for mental health in sports, finding a renewed sense of mission. In your case, what initially felt like an abyss can become fertile ground to plant the seeds of a new vision for yourself.

Your story is far from over after that big success. In fact, this might be the moment when the *truest* part of your story begins – the part where *you* (not external expectations) define what a good life looks like. Take a moment to imagine what you want the next few years to be about. If there were chapters ahead titled "My Most Fulfilling Days," what would be happening in them? Perhaps you see yourself exploring a creative pursuit that you never had time for before. Perhaps you imagine dedicating time to causes that move your heart, or strengthening the foundations of your personal life that were neglected during your climb to the top. Whatever that vision is, let it come from your deepest values and interests. The emptiness you felt is simply the space in which this new purpose can take root. Like a clearing after a forest fire, it may look desolate at first, but it is exactly where fresh growth is poised to emerge.

As you step forward with this new mindset, remember that the end of one journey is the exciting beginning of another. You stand *beyond the finish line* now, looking ahead with hard-won wisdom. You know now that external success, while sweet, is not the ultimate reward – the real reward is a life lived meaningfully each day. Armed with that knowledge, you can venture into your future without the old illusions. Instead of chasing validation, you can chase *fulfillment*. Instead of fearing the void, you can embrace it as possibility. With purpose and wholeness as your guiding stars, the road ahead is not something to dread – it's something to eagerly anticipate. In many ways, your best and most fulfilling days may well lie ahead of you, not behind. Each day is an opportunity to write the next chapter in a story only you can tell. So take a deep breath, feel the solid ground of *now* beneath your feet, and step forward. The summit you conquered was never meant to be a final ending – it was a milestone that has prepared you for the journeys to come. With your vision in hand and your values in heart, begin the next ascent. The journey continues, and this time, you know *exactly* what true success means to you.

Open and optimistic, you move forward – beyond the finish line, where a whole new horizon awaits.

Epilogue

As the final page turns, you're left with an undeniable truth: the journey doesn't end at the summit. That peak, once a shining beacon of success, might no longer feel as fulfilling as you thought it would. The accolades, the recognition, the material rewards—all of it can feel hollow when the excitement fades and the applause quiets. It's not failure, though; it's the natural consequence of living for achievements alone.

But there's a silver lining—this chapter of your life doesn't have to be about searching for a new "high" or chasing another fleeting victory. It's about redefining who you are beyond what you've done. You've climbed mountains, faced challenges, and broken barriers. Now, it's time to discover the more profound parts of you, the parts that have always been there but might have been overshadowed by the need for external validation.

Finding purpose after "making it" isn't about seeking an answer in accomplishments. It's about the journey of self-discovery, the quiet spaces where your true passions, relationships, and sense of meaning reside. Rebuilding your identity doesn't require monumental change; sometimes it's as simple as giving yourself the permission to be, to breathe, and to grow without the weight of achievement driving you.

As you move forward, remember this: you are not your past success. The best part of your story has yet to be written. New adventures, new challenges, and new growth await. There is beauty in the spaces between achievements, where you can reconnect with the joy of living, of being present, and of cultivating purpose in ways that transcend the limits of success. You've already made it, but now, the real journey begins. And it's going to be more rewarding than you ever imagined.